Future Daddy

The Ultimate Guide for First-Time Dads

Andres Mooring

Table of Contents

Introduction

"Anyone who tells you fatherhood is the greatest thing that can happen to you, they are understating it." - Mike Myers

So you and your wife/girlfriend are pregnant? That must feel really exciting! But what is that feeling at the bottom of your heart that feels more like dread than exhilaration?

If you are anything like I was during my wife's first pregnancy, you must be close to panicking at the prospect of raising another human being. It doesn't help that all the pregnancy material out there only addresses issues that women go through during pregnancy. All your questions, all your worries and all your concerns go unanswered. And of course, your role in the pregnancy was not over as soon as your baby was conceived! The next nine months will be a rehearsal for the lifelong role you will be playing now—you will be a father.

I really wish that someone had written me a book when I was preparing for the birth of my daughter. It was a time filled with uncertainties and doubts, and yet the material I found online was grossly insufficient to boost my confidence in my ability to take care of a family. I mean, how are you supposed to step to the plate if you don't even know what is going on? You need dependable information to kill that voice of doubt that has been nagging at the back of your brain. You need to know that you can handle everything coming your way for your excitement to take root.

Only when you have the proper information will you be in a position to show up and crush this pregnancy like the dependable man that you are. Parenting actually starts at pregnancy, and understanding everything that is about to happen—including the disruptions that this baby will bring to your life—will make you a better father. Your significant other needs all the love and support that you can give her because her health is inextricably linked to the health of your baby. But you need to know *how* to give this love and support.

In this book, I have laid out the facts as I learned them during my two pregnancies. Within the following seven chapters are practical skills on handling different aspects of baby care as a father. I have thrown in a few useful tips to help you along, as well, and incorporated tried and tested techniques in every single chapter. With this book, you will understand exactly what is expected of you from day one of pregnancy to taking care of the infant in the coming months.

See, the world at large associates pregnancy with motherhood. Pretty much every book out there deals with the mommy side of it and neglects the daddy side of it. New dads are left to fend for themselves and hardly get the same attention, yet they play an ever-increasing role in birthing as well as caring for a newborn. In fact, even relatives and loved ones tend to focus on mom and baby after the birth. Fathers often feel left out, like an unwanted third wheel, in a very special relationship. This often leads to distance and isolation and negative impacts on the relationships with both mother and child.

It doesn't help that the chauvinistic institution of manhood fosters little support from fellow men. Beyond the "Yeah, the night might be a little tough" response, most men are not exactly raring to talk about their experiences. So, even as you seek the support of your peers, you might find that their help isn't all that useful. New dads experience an emotional roller coaster of supporting a pregnancy wife/girlfriend and the pressure of added responsibility in caring for two people. The other source of stress comes from the additional financial responsibility and being unable to care for the baby as well as the mother.

The scarcity of literature teaching fathers about what to expect during pregnancy means that most are too overcome with fears and doubts at birth to form an instant connection. Talking about the birth of his son, one father tells of how his wife was overcome with love at first sight as soon as she saw the newborn. All he could come up with, in the meantime, was, "He seems nice." Hardly something you'd expect a father to say about his very own baby, but most fathers don't always feel immediately bonded to their children at birth. There is a good chance that you will resent the changes and the chaos the baby brings in the first weeks or months. But in time you will inevitably feel what every dad feels—that you would give your life for your baby.

Another huge issue for fathers is a sense of detachment from the whole affair. A mother, having carried the baby for nine months, is emotionally, physically, and mentally vested from the word go. The father, on the other hand, has to try to feel the same emotions as the wife. And there is no guarantee that you will succeed. Studies have shown that fathers don't always have an immediate bond like the one women experience after the birth of a child. That is why a new dad would say something like "he seems nice."

What you need to understand about your love for the baby and your wife's love is this: your love is learned, but hers is granted. If you don't want to feel that disenchanted "he seems nice" kind of feeling when welcoming your child into the world, it may help to become more involved in the pregnancy.

As a father of two, I dare say that I have a wealth of knowledge on fatherhood. I believe that fathers can enjoy fatherhood and deal with the confusion and chaos it brings a lot better if they first build their understanding of this crucial time. More than for just the practical aspects of fathering a baby, I have written this book to help you deal with the emotional uncertainty that new dads go through, as well as the changing relationship with your partner. So, strap down and take out your notebook. You are about to get daddy schooled!

Chapter 1:

What to Expect When She's Expecting

Preparations for the birth of a child should start long before the actual event. And if you want to improve your chances of developing a more instantaneous connection to the baby, being more involved in the pregnancy is your best bet. I believe that part of the reason why fathers have difficulties connecting with their newborns is that they invest minimal time and energy in the pregnancy. At the same time, you are dealing with so many uncertainties and so much fear that it may be hard for you to feel anything but dread.

This chapter starts us off in the journey that begins with finding out that your partner is pregnant. Whether the pregnancy is planned or unplanned, you will never forget your first time. Especially the moment when it finally dawns on you that your entire life is about to change and nothing will ever be the same again. But don't freak out, parenting can be fun and fulfilling—if you know what you are doing.

Understanding Pregnancy

As excited as you both are about starting a family, chances are that this excitement will wear off as you get closer to the big day. For your woman, the coming nine months will be anything but enjoyable. She will have to deal with nausea, ligament pain, bloating, and weight gain, not to mention the labor pains at the end of this road. You get the better half of the stick. Other than the anxiety of fatherhood, you will be just as good physically when you find out that you are an expectant father as you will be six months into the pregnancy... well, unless you gain weight along with your mate.

That is why you have to start thinking even more than before about your girlfriend's/wife's welfare now that she is building a new life inside her. You will also have to organize your life to make it possible for you to fulfill your parental responsibilities. This is a "for her and for him" guide to pregnancy. And remember, the biggest role you play as a father during pregnancy is supporting your wife/girlfriend. For the next nine months, you are the only robust member of this three-member club. You will have to do not most, but ALL of the heavy lifting.

But even more important is to gain a deeper understanding of the changes going on during this time.

What happens to your partner and your baby during the pregnancy?

First Trimester

The first trimester lasts from the first week to week thirteen and entails the baby growing from one fertilized egg into a fully formed fetus. By the end, your baby will be capable of movement, with the arms, legs, and fingers starting to develop. Muscles and blood cells will start to form in the first trimester as the baby starts developing its own immune system.

Because of the massive hormonal activity going on within her, your partner will experience morning sickness from around the sixth week. However, the nausea does not occur in the morning only. It is not uncommon for a woman to experience it at all times of the day.

Perhaps the more disruptive change taking place in the first trimester will be the mood swings. At one moment she will be in high spirits, then crying the next moment, and back to crushing sadness the next. It might be even more serious if your partner has a history of depressive behaviors or if the mood swings are too severe.

Beware if your partner has heavy vaginal bleeding at this time or complains of abdominal pains. It might be an indication of possible complications and needs the attention of a doctor as soon as possible.

Second Trimester

The second trimester starts in the fourteenth week and goes until the twenty-seventh. After the hormonal strain of the first trimester, it is a time of relative peace for the mother. In the second trimester, the baby becomes even more active, as it develops bodily functions. At about four and a half months (week 18), the baby is able to yawn and hiccup. All those muscles and organs that started developing in the first trimester kick into high gear during the second. You can feel the heart beating at around week twenty, and by week twenty-six you can expect the all-exciting kicks to begin.

For your woman, this can be a stressful time marred by swollen feet and ankles. Her legs may also cramp unexpectedly, especially if she has a shortage of magnesium and calcium. Pregnant ladies are also most likely to put on a lot of weight at this point in the pregnancy. This may bring another issue—body image. You will have to be extra sensitive so as not to upset her and also to make her feel beautiful and loved.

The second trimester is considerably less risky compared to the first, but this does not mean that there are no risks. Persistent abdominal pains, high fever, and heavy vaginal bleeding mean that you have to get your wife/girlfriend checked out. Another issue that might develop in the second trimester and cause concern for you and your wife/girlfriend is gestational diabetes. You will need to get tested at about the twenty-sixth week.

Third Trimester

In the third trimester, your baby will finish the last development stages of in-utero growth. This period starts in the twenty-eighth week and lasts through the fortieth, although it is not uncommon for a baby to come early or late. Even though your baby enters the third trimester with its features fully formed, it still does a lot of growing in this period. In fact, the baby grows from about 2.5 pounds at the start to between six and nine pounds at birth.

In this period, the baby converts all the cartilage it has formed to this point into bones. This requires a lot of calcium consumption. At the thirty-fourth week of the pregnancy, your baby will usually turn and face the cervix in readiness for exiting the womb. This makes exiting easier. But if the position change does not occur, the doctor will simply turn the fetus around during birth.

You should look out for Braxton Hicks contractions during these last few months. They are simply run-ups to the real labor coming soon. And because your wife/girlfriend is now lugging a fully formed baby inside her, you can expect her fatigue levels to hit crazy new heights. It is important to compensate for all this energy use with proper dieting and supplements where necessary.

Your Role in the Pregnancy

Three or four generations ago, it was virtually impossible to find a man who involved himself in the birthing process. Women were left to tend to their own needs by themselves—probably with the help of a sympathetic female relative. Men were distant spectators who wouldn't be caught dead lingering around or in the delivery room. But times have changed and men are more involved in pregnancy now. You don't have to act all macho and act like you don't care what is going on inside your wife. You would probably help your wife/girlfriend carry the baby if you could, but since that is biologically impossible, here are a few things you can do to help her through this time.

Be Her Sidekick

You are starting (or continuing) to build a family, so you are in this together. Support her and assist her in whatever she needs help with. Ask, don't wait for her to tell you what needs to happen. If you can anticipate her needs before she has them, you will make her time a lot easier. Think of this season as a journey or an adventure that you are taking together. She is the lead (obviously) and you are the sidekick. Play that role well and you are guaranteed to win a supporting role award for being the best partner/father ever!

One of the best ways to support your partner during this time is to give her the opportunity to talk about the pregnancy with someone who is as emotionally invested in it as she is. Let her talk about the changes taking place in her body, talk about your expectations, and discuss baby names. Just beware of those mood swings, because you will definitely experience them. One moment she will be cool and chatty, and the next moment she zips up and doesn't want to see your face. You will have to take it all in stride.

You must also learn how to support your partner. As her belly grows, she will become increasingly dependent on you for everyday things. Some of them might be very mundane, but you will still have to do them. The more supportive you are of her, the better a time she will have with the pregnancy—and the healthier your son/daughter will be when born. One great thing about being the sidekick in your partner's pregnancy is that you don't have to fear showing her up. She is the star of this show and nothing you do can take that away from her. All the same, you must remember that everything you are doing is meant to be in support.

Emotional Support

Pregnancy will be a stressful time for you, but not nearly as stressful as it will be for your partner. With the hormone-induced mood swings and the changes occurring in her body, she will need the emotional support of her man. Reassure her constantly and celebrate her body as the magical crucible it really is. One way you can help her forget about all these changes in her body is to direct her focus to the magic of a life forming inside her. Talk to the baby, listen to the tiny heartbeat, and experience those kicks with her. These are also the things that make men appreciate the magic of birth and appreciate their babies as soon as they are born rather than resenting them as I mentioned in the introduction.

And to make sure that you keep up with everything going on with her body during this time, ensure that you go with her to as many doctor appointments as you can. This way, you will also stay on top of all the developments with the baby as well. If you can, you should also consider taking birth and newborn care classes together. You might be one of the few (or the only) men in the class, but you will learn a whole lot of useful stuff from it. And the fact that you are learning all about baby care with your wife strengthens the bond you share, reassures her of your support, and empowers you to be a great dad in the future.

Man Up

Pregnancy is a time when even the handiest woman becomes very inept at performing even mildly strenuous physical activities. And yet there is a lot of stuff the baby needs that your house will probably be lacking. It falls 100% upon you to do all these things. Just know that however strenuous these activities may get, they do not come close to the kind of physical strain your partner feels carrying the baby throughout the whole pregnancy.

Your home must have all the things needed to welcome the new addition to the family comfortably. It falls upon you to give your house the once-over and determine if there is enough space for when the baby comes. How baby-friendly is your house, your neighborhood, and your part of the city? Throughout the pregnancy and after the baby comes, it is always best if you have a hospital and a grocery store close by in the event that you need something quickly. If you don't have enough space, start searching for a bigger house with all the amenities your family needs close by.

There will be a lot of lugging and hauling, purchasing and installing all the baby essentials you need to integrate the baby into your life. You will need things like a crib, a car seat, diapers, clothes, toys, hygiene products, etc. Some of these things, like a crib, you will have to build (or at least assemble) yourself while others you can just buy from the store and place them where they are needed.

And as you build or assemble the crib, you will also have to get the nursery ready. Building the nursery may entail simple tasks like painting the room or more complicated ones like building toy racks and a wardrobe. If you are not handy with tools, you can pay a professional to build all these things. But it will give you great joy to do all these things yourself, so don't be too eager to pass on these activities to the cheapest carpenter on craigslist.

Even though the baby will not be moving around the house for at least a year after birth, there is no harm in getting the house ready for it in advance. Start identifying the potentially problematic sections of the house and figuring out ways of fixing them. Your house should be baby-proofed for as long as there is a baby in the house. Moreover, if you do it now, you will have more time to enjoy your baby's growth later on instead of rushing to get the house ready.

Part of getting your house ready for the baby entails reimagining spaces like the kitchen. As soon as the baby comes, you will have scores of baby care supplies like bottles, baby food-making equipment, milk pumps, and utensils. You need to clean out some of the redundant items in the kitchen to make way for all these. The countertop, the fridge, and drawers are some of the areas that will require alterations to make room for the baby. Just keep in mind that the kitchen is often the woman's domain. In fact, in my experience, women usually feel territorial about any space within the house. So be careful about making any changes without consulting with her. She may not have the physical strength or motivation to help with the changes, but I assure you that she may have strong opinions!

Sex During Pregnancy

If you have been trying to get pregnant for a while, then you have probably been getting extra frisky for some time. But what happens now that you are pregnant? You can still keep the flames of your intimacy over the next nine months. Or maybe it is not possible; it all depends on how the pregnancy affects your partner. Let's delve a little deeper into that, shall we?

When Is It Safe?

For most couples, sex will be safe and pleasurable throughout the term of the pregnancy. Only in some very special circumstances may your doctor advise you against doing it. Some of these circumstances include if your partner has a history of going into labor prematurely or if there are signs of a possible premature birth. This is because sex has been thought to be an effective way of inducing labor. Another reason why your doctor might recommend you don't have sex is in the event that your cervix is not healthy enough to accommodate penetration. In all these circumstances, your doctor will advise you on the way forward.

In normal circumstances, it is perfectly safe to have sex during pregnancy, as the baby is usually protected inside the cervix by a mucus plug. There is no way for the penis to get through this and disturb the baby. But you do have to mind her comfort, especially when her stomach swells in the second and third trimesters. This requires that you adapt to more comfortable sexual positions.

Missionary position would only work if you can hold yourself off and not put your weight on her. However, being on her back for extended periods of time might be uncomfortable for your partner. In this case, it is better to have her on top where she can control the depth and pace of penetration. Side-by-side sex is also a perfect way to go at it, as you are both lying on the bed and can go at it for as long as you want. The only thing you must NEVER do is cunnilingus where you blow air inside her (if you are into that sort of thing). This tends to cause air embolism, which can be quite dangerous.

Common Myths

There is a lot of misinformation about the impact of sex during pregnancy out there. Below is a list of five common ones.

1. You can harm the fetus if you go too deep.

This is a nonsensical claim, with no basis whatsoever, that you need to disregard at all costs. The vagina stretches during sex and creates a huge gap between your penis and the uterus. Regardless of how well-endowed you are, there is no way you are going to break through the mucus plug protecting the baby or the amniotic sac in which it is suspended.

2. An orgasm can lead to miscarriage.

Female orgasms entail the contracting of vaginal muscles, but this will have no impact on the baby whatsoever. First off, the amniotic sac absorbs all of this pressure. Secondly, the contractions of an orgasm are very different from the birth pains that lead to preterm birth (miscarriage). The former are pleasurable and brief while the latter are painful and occur in intervals of about five minutes.

3. Sex will induce labor.

This is a widely held belief, but it has not been proven. While semen does contain the prostaglandin hormone that aids in stimulating labor, the chemical composition of this hormone may be too mild to have a powerful-enough effect. Still, there are many couples who will tell stories of having been intimate within a day of going into labor.

4. The baby can feel it as well

Cocooned in its protective sac and locked away in the uterus, the baby remains oblivious to the outside world all throughout pregnancy. Even though it can feel the motion of what you are doing, there is no way of differentiating between sex and other forms of motion like walking. For all it knows, mama is just taking a very brisk walk. There is no way for the baby to interpret your actions anyway, because it does not have the knowledge or point of reference.

5. ALL blood is bad

Women have been known to experience some blood flow during pregnancy, especially during or after sex. This does not mean that she is broken or that you hurt her. It is simply a result of tenderness in the cervix, which opens up the capillaries at the lightest touch. As long as there is no pain and the blood is only light, there is no reason to quit doing *it*.

Special Considerations

As healthy and safe as it might be, sex during pregnancy has to be very considerate to the needs of your partner. You have to listen to her even more than ever before. Below are some tips to make sure that you don't mess up or miss out in these crucial times.

Flow with the tide

With the strain her body is going through as she builds a new person within her, your partner is likely to move from moments of extreme exhaustion and no sexual appetite to high energy and extreme horniness. You will have to accommodate her. So, in the moments when she just wants to sleep, ask whether she wants to cuddle. And when she wants to pull an all-nighter, well, just hope that you are up to the task! Just make sure that you both still manage to get some sleep so that you can continue being on top of your game in all other areas of your lives.

Give it a try in the second trimester

If you are lucky, your partner will be sexually charged for the whole nine months of her pregnancy. However, chances are that she will lose her libido to the morning sickness and the anxiety of the first trimester and be too exhausted to give it a go in the third. This leaves the second trimester as the moment when her body is best primed for some good old tumble in the sheets.

Don't worry about hurting her or the baby

If you worry too much that you might hurt your partner or the baby, you might have trouble performing in the sack. You need to understand that the baby is well protected and that you can no more hurt her now than you could before she got pregnant. Sometimes there might be a tinge of blood after sex, but this is only because her uterus is more sensitive. The same hormones that make her more horny and ready for sex will be the same hormones inducing this slight bleeding. Unless the blood becomes too much, there is no need to panic.

YOUR Emotional Health

Fatherhood can be very stressful for some dads. Your whole life is about to change in ways that you can only imagine, and you are probably afraid that you will be a terrible father. This is a good thing—no bad father ever worried about the kind of job they were doing in raising their kids. If you are worried, then it means that you are more likely to seek to learn and take your duties more seriously. You may also be comforted to know that hardly anyone goes through fatherhood without some serious dread and anxiety.

Yet you will now be expected to take on responsibilities you have never taken on before, starting with caring for your partner through the pregnancy and then your child later on. All these responsibilities are the kind that require commitment and dedication. But most importantly, you must take good care of yourself first. You cannot fulfill your parental responsibilities if you don't first take care of your own emotional needs. In this section, we will look at some stress areas that you should cover.

Deal With Your Parenting Anxieties

To take good care of your emotional health, you must start by processing your feelings about fatherhood.

What kind of father do you think you will be? What kind of father do you want to be? If you had a great father, you can simply model your parenting style after him. You can make some alterations to the things you disliked about him. Or maybe your father was not the best role model and you want to be completely different. And that is okay too. The important thing is defining the kind of dad that you want to be. This way, you have a definitive measure against which you can measure your performance when the baby comes.

It helps to talk to your partner about the kind of parents that you would like to be as a team. There is a good chance that she is feeling the same kind of anxieties that you are feeling, and talking about your anxieties will help her deal with the fears she is too terrified to face on her own. Confronting fears is the first step in overcoming them. As soon as you do this, you will have empowered yourself to step up and take on the forthcoming responsibilities in a commanding manner.

Take Care of the Financials

Whatever else pregnancy will be for you and your partner; you can bet that it will be a financially stressful time. Of all the strains that fatherhood places on you, money is one of the biggest issues. You need to figure out a way of providing for your baby's needs in advance. Baby products are a lot more expensive than you might have guessed and there are A LOT of them needed. And I am not talking about "it would be great to have that one" kind of needed, I am talking "the baby absolutely NEEDS this!" From diapers to baby foods, supplements, car seats, a bed, etc., you will have to shell out a lot of money over the next few years.

If you are not financially capable, you are inviting trouble into your life with the impending birth of your baby. If you have any money worries, it is important that you address them before the pregnancy. As soon as you have a sufficient amount saved up for everything you will need, your mind will be more at ease and you can properly anticipate the coming of your baby.

Physical Health

You need to keep your body in top physical health to be able to take proper care of your expectant wife and make those preparations for the baby. Remember, you will be doing all the heavy lifting around the house for the next nine months. It would be very inconvenient if you hurt yourself or are too tired to step up. Do not stop your morning run or hitting the gym just because your partner is pregnant. In fact, unless the doctor orders it, neither should she. You both need your health to be perfect over the coming months. Motivate each other to eat right and have enough sleep every night.

Guidance

If you fear that you might get overwhelmed (or you are already overwhelmed now), then you could profit from some guidance. Talk to people who already have some fatherhood experience and who can give you adequate information about the things that trouble you right now.

You probably have a friend or two with babies who will be eager to impart some of their wisdom on baby care. Of course, you must only take advice from dads that you admire. No need listening to someone whose parenting style turns you off. Find that one dad you know who has the most admirable parenting style and invite him for a beer and pick his brain—it will take you a long way.

To Dos

In the coming nine months, you will have to step up and do some things that you have always relied on your wife/girlfriend to do. In this chapter, I will lay out a month-by-month guide to some of the fatherly duties you must take up over the period of the pregnancy.

First Trimester

The first trimester is a time of mixed emotions and massive hormonal changes.

First month

In the first month, you are excited about finding out that you are pregnant. There are probably no visible changes save for the onset of morning sickness. This is a time when you can still go out—if she is up to it—and have some fun.

As early as now, visit the HR department at the office and familiarize yourself with your employer's policies on paternity benefits, such as paid time off. Also make sure you understand how your medical coverage will pay (or not) for necessary or preferred care.

Make the first step in becoming an involved dad by taking on one job around the house to relieve your partner. It can be as small as folding the laundry or cooking, but it will lessen her load and earn you some baby daddy points.

Second month

As the second month rolls around, pick up more jobs around the house that you can consistently. Your partner's body is spending increasingly more of her energy growing the baby inside her, which means that she is likely to be exhausted all the time. Whatever you are doing right now, you can do even more to help out.

You should also start thinking about the godparents at this time. Godparents are the ones who will assume guardianship of your child should you and your mate experience any unfortunate event. Pick the closest friends or family members that you know will do a good job raising your child.

Indulge her pregnancy quirks. She will request (or demand) specific foods or her old food prepared a specifically odd way. Let her have it her way as much as possible, even if you would not go close to her cravings.

Third month

This is the month where you can hear your baby's heart beating, so be sure to attend the doctor's checkup at any cost. After the doctor's appointment, take her out to dinner and gush together about your tiny bundle of joy.

Now that her baby bump is beginning to show, tell her she looks beautiful. She is probably feeling self-conscious about the extra weight she has been picking up, so this is very important. But choose your words wisely. It will do you no good to use words like "big" or "rounding up."

Second Trimester

The second trimester is often accompanied by more energy and voracious appetite. However, every week and every month will bring its own set of challenges.

Fourth month

Set aside an allowance for the baby. Transfer all your baby savings into this account and allocate a portion of your monthly income to go there as well. The better financially prepared you are, the better off you will be emotionally as you count down to the birth of the baby.

Engage in a pregnancy workout with your partner. Exercising has been found to have some very positive health benefits for expectancy. Even a simple walk around the neighborhood will help your partner to stay healthy and cheerful.

Fifth month

The fifth month is a great time to take a vacation, especially because she can't fly in the third trimester. Take this time to have a pre-baby-moon, just the two of you, since you might never get another opportunity in a very long time. Just select those destinations that will not be too strenuous for her, like the beach or a luxury hotel in her favorite city.

Hit the stores or online retailers and stock up on baby supplies together. By now you probably know the gender of your baby, so you can shop for gender-specific baby items. Whether or not you can do the shopping alone, the experience will bond you together as parents in a huge way. Do not miss out by sending her out with her girlfriends.

If you haven't done so already, this is the time to plan for the child's future care. Discuss whether one of you should stay at home (and who it will be) or if you will both go back to work. Think about reliable baby care as well. Can you afford to pay a private nanny or will you resort to a daycare center? Decide all these things in advance to make the transition back into your lives as smooth as possible.

Sixth month

Fix everything that needs fixing around the house. If you have any pending repairs, renovations, or construction projects that you want to do before the baby comes, this is the perfect time for them. For example, you can complete the crib and the nursery after work and over the weekend.

Take her out and treat her to a spectacular evening. She may be exhausted all the time now, but she will be even more so in the coming months. If you want to enjoy a night out together, this might be your last chance in a long time. Go wherever she wants to go, even if it would be your last choice for a date night. Make her feel special and make her breakfast in bed for full measure!

Third Trimester

As the third trimester rolls around, your baby is now fully formed and she can even hear you talking to him/her. Your partner's moods, in the meantime, are swinging more wildly than ever. It's going to be a tough couple of months.

Seventh month

Whether you want it or not, you will have to take over running the house. Your partner is probably too absentminded to do much of anything by now, so you will either bring in a friend or relative to cook and look after her, or you will have to step up yourself.

Give your entire baby game a once-over. You should be pretty well prepared for the baby by now, but what if you are missing something? In just a month or so, you will be welcoming your baby into the world. If there is anything that you have left out, it is high time that you get it sorted out as soon as possible.

Eighth month

Start packing for the emergency room. By now you are probably doing so much that you cannot imagine there being anything more to do. But you still have to pack an overnight bag for the inevitable rush to the hospital. Don't forget to pack for your own supplies, unless you want to leave her alone in the delivery room to charge your phone midway through delivery.

Reassure each other. It is getting so close to the big date, huh? How are you feeling? Nervous? Me too! These will probably be the last few months of quiet nights you will ever share if your baby is not a sound sleeper (which is very likely). Enjoy some long talks and cuddle time, and be each other's center of attention before the baby comes.

Ninth month

In the final month of pregnancy, you just know that the labor pains may start at any moment. It is absolutely critical that you stay on top of everything now. Give your house and baby supplies a final once-over and stock up on any last-minute shopping, including diapers and baby food.

To prepare for the not-too-distant future when your baby starts crawling, take a belly-crawl around the house and take note of the loose objects and wires that might harm an innocent soul. Take care of any baby proofing that you might have previously overlooked now. Any day now you will be hightailing it to the delivery room.

Chapter 2:

Baby's Birth and Beyond

The days around the birth of your child are going to be probably the most stressful days of your life. Before the baby comes, you will be looking out for any indication of the onset of labor. Waiting becomes especially stressful if your baby does not come out at the 9-month mark. During birth, you will probably be feeling out of your depth, surrounded by doctors and nurses at the delivery room. If you opt to remain outside, the wait (which can stretch for hours) will be unbearable. After your baby is born, you will have to balance between making sure everything at home is ready for the arrival of the new family member while spending as much time as possible in the hospital sharing in the joy of your newborn with your partner. In this chapter, we will discuss the activities involved in helping your partner bring your baby into the world.

Preparing for Delivery

As you move closer to the due date, there are two big-picture questions that you will need to settle. They include the type of birth you will have and your role or level of participation in the birth of your child.

The Type of Birth You Will Have

There are two primary methods of giving birth, namely vaginal and cesarean. Choosing which method to use in bringing your child into the world depends on personal preferences, doctor's recommendation, and extenuating factors during the actual birth.

Vaginal birth

Vaginal delivery is any form of birth in which a child comes into the world through the birth canal. There are several types of vaginal birth, including epidural, assisted, and natural.

With an epidural, a woman receives pain medication to give some relief during the otherwise excruciating process of childbirth. In an epidural birth, local anesthesia is introduced into the body through the base of the spinal cord. The local anesthesia gives a woman total relief from the pains of contractions and makes for a relatively painless birth. Some side effects include delayed onset of the second phase of labor and, in some cases, losing the ability to push. Your doctor will advise you on this procedure if you and your partner opt for it, including whether she is eligible (not every woman can receive an epidural).

Methods of assisted vaginal birth include the use of vacuum and forceps. The decision to bring in an extra tool (the assistance) is usually made when the woman is, for whatever reasons, unable to keep pushing to pass the baby through the birth canal. Sometimes it can be due to exhaustion or simply because the baby is taking too long. Assisted births can be lifesaving too, especially when they are used to hasten delivery amid health concerns for the mother and/or the baby.

With a vacuum birth, a specialized vacuum extractor is used to gently pull the baby out. A vacuumed cup is placed on the baby's crowning head. Even with a very low suction capability, this cup still allows the doctor to gently guide the baby out. It can also be used alongside the woman's own efforts, giving every push more power because there is some extra force being applied on the outwards motion of the baby. Vacuum extractions are most effective from the second stage of birth because the baby is a lot lower in the pelvis.

With a forceps-assisted birth, the doctor will use specialized forceps, much like tongs, to help clear a path for the baby to come out by manually widening the vagina. Only trained obstetricians may use forceps in the birthing process and only to speed up a stalled birth or hasten delivery to avert a medical emergency.

Natural birth is a special type of vaginal delivery in which the entire process proceeds without resorting to any form of invasive therapy or medical procedures of any sort. Although natural birth may be tougher, it allows for the most natural process of birthing possible and enhances the bond between mother and child. In natural delivery, the focus is placed on the process of pushing to birth the child, with special consideration being given to positions and exercises for the utmost level of comfort for the mother. Some specialized methods of natural delivery include water birthing, whereby a woman delivers in a warm-water tub with the help of a midwife. This method allows for a gentler, more natural birthing experience, with the water's buoyancy providing some level of pain relief for the mother.

Caesarean birth

Caesarean, or C-section, birth entails the making of an incision in the stomach wall and through the uterus to create a new path for the baby to come out. Delivering a child by caesarean section foregoes the whole process of birthing through the vaginal canal. Because it is a surgical procedure, an anesthesia will be used, either general or localized from the waist downwards. In the latter, the woman is at least able to see the baby after delivery, even if she will be bedridden for days afterwards.

Caesarean birth may be used when a mother decides to forego the whole vaginal canal birthing procedure, when there are problems with the baby or the mother that rules out vaginal birth, or in the event of an emergency. Up to 30% of births in America are taking place through C-section birth now partly because it is necessary and partly because doctors recommend it more. Yet while this might be the least painful of all methods of birthing, it is not necessarily the best.

Choosing your method of delivery

Delivering through the vaginal canal is considered more beneficial to both the mother and the child. The process of being pushed through the narrow vaginal canal helps in getting the baby's internal organs to work. For example, vaginal birthing squeezes fluids out of a baby's lungs, reducing the chances of the child developing breathing problems later in life. Moreover, the process of birth gives the baby an immune boost by exposing it to good bacteria in the vaginal tract.

Because the mother's pain and physical difficulties end immediately after birth, she will be in a position to hold the baby and start breastfeeding very soon afterwards.

This skin-to-skin contact between mother and baby is very beneficial. It signals to the mother to start producing milk for the baby, which means that breastfeeding starts sooner rather than later. The only (unlikely) downside to vaginal birthing is that bigger babies may suffer some bruises or fractures.

With a caesarean birth, the only benefit is scheduling the date of your child's birth. However, the recovery time after birth will be longer, and the woman will experience discomforts long after birth. Future births will also have to consider the potential harm they might put on the old scar. Furthermore, caesarean birth increases the chances of a child developing breathing problems and childhood obesity.

Verdict: if at all plausible, always go for the vaginal methods of birthing, whether assisted or natural. The only reason to resort to caesarean birth is if birthing through the vaginal canal would pose some serious risks to the mother or the baby.

Yet, bear in mind that the primary authority in this decision rests with the mother. It's her body, after all, and she knows best what she is capable of enduring or not. If you and your woman do not agree about the best way for her to give birth, this is an important opportunity for you to grow in the maturity and selflessness that a good father requires. Find a way to support her and embrace her decision as though it is your own.

Your Level of Participation

Even as you discuss the best delivery style with your partner, there is another important issue that *you* must address—where you will be through it all. In the olden days, the place of the man would always be outside the delivery room, pacing anxiously as the woman did all the heavy lifting inside. Nowadays, you can be right by your partner's side through this time if you want to— but more importantly, if she wants you there. Not all women appreciate the company of their partner during birth. In some cases, she might even resent you during the labor pains and throw you out.

That is why you should have the talk with your partner and decide what role you will play during the birth of your baby well in advance. The only rule here, as with most other things during pregnancy, is that your woman has the final say. If she wants you out, you stay out. If she wants you by her side, then by all means that is where you should be. Your job will always be as her unrelenting supporter at this time.

First Stage of Labor

At the end of the nine months comes the most physically tasking process for your partner yet—

delivery. The entire process lasts from eight to eighteen hours, divided into four phases. In the first stage of labor, the cervix thins and starts to open up in readiness for the baby passing through. This is the cause of all the contractions that a woman feels.

The first stage of labor is the most important because it starts in the house, which means that you will have a bigger role to play in getting your partner safely through and on to the hands of the professionals who will help her through the latter stages. And even though your partner probably already knows how to recognize the beginnings of her labor, it is important that you learn to recognize the onset too. The last thing you want to be is the partner who does not have a clue what is going on or what is needed of him, including at that moment of pre-delivery room madness at home. The following are the things you should wait for before you load your delivery room bags into your car and hightail it to the hospital.

Early Labor

Early labor starts a few days before a woman is due to give birth as her body prepares for the actual birthing. It entails:

Lightening

When your baby is ready for delivery, it will drop from its location near the ribcage and come to rest deep in the pelvis with the head facing downwards. This is the very last stage of the baby's development, occurring a few weeks or a few days before labor begins. After the baby drops, your partner will start to breathe more easily because the baby is not pressed up against her diaphragm. However, due to the added pressure of a full-grown baby pressing against her bladder, she might also get the urge to urinate a lot more frequently than before.

Nesting instinct

In some cases, when the baby drops and a woman gets more freedom to move (or waddle) about, she becomes very active in making preparations for the arrival of the baby. This is called the nesting instinct and it kicks in with an inexhaustible burst of energy, even for a woman who has been too exhausted to do anything throughout the pregnancy.

Passing the mucus plug

In the days leading up to the actual birth of the baby, it is common for women to experience an increase in the volume of their vaginal discharge. This includes the mucus plug that blocks off the uterus from the vagina. Although the mucus plug may be pushed out of the body a few days before birth, it is also not unheard of for a woman to release it just a few hours before birth. Of course, you will only learn about this if you are an active participant in the pregnancy and the birthing process. Your partner won't be inclined to share this particular event with you unless you care about knowing everything.

What to do

At the onset of labor, your woman will probably be too confused or in too much pain to take care of herself. If ever there was a time that you needed to step up, then the onset of labor (and what follows afterward) is it. Chances are that you will not be too sure of what is going on or what is expected of you during this time. Even after having taken a birthing class, you will probably still be a little confused as to what you need to do at any given time.

First off, no matter how tempting it might be, don't rush to the hospital right away. If she is not ready yet, (if her labor is in the latent stage) the nurses will just keep you waiting around or send you back home. Waiting around the hospital is more stressful because of the unfamiliarity and the lack of home comforts like food, drink, and free movement. Unless your doctor or your wife asks you to take her to the hospital, wait until she gets to the end of the latent phase of labor before making the trip. But only do this if the hospital is not more than ten minutes or so away. If the trip is a little longer, then you are safer just packing a hospital bag and waiting around the hospital for the baby to come.

In the meantime, you should help monitor the contractions, especially if you have a contraction monitor. Just talking her through the peaks and the dips in the pain will give her a sense of control and will go a long way in calming her down. Dote on her and make sure that she is as comfortable as she can possibly be.

Pack a hospital bag

A hospital bag is very important to ensure the best possible level of comfort for your partner and you during your time at the hospital. The items that should not be missing in this bag include:

- A comfortable robe for your partner.
- All the toiletries she needs. Be sure to ask her and help her trim down to the basics if she wants to bring her whole collection of beauty products.
- Comfortable clothes for both of you. You may decide to put your clothes in a separate bag for easier access, but it is absolutely important that you both have comfortable clothes.
- Bring along some water for drinking in a reusable container. The process of birthing

(especially pushing) is very exhausting. Your wife will probably need it for afterwards.

- If the wait turns out to be longer than just a few hours, you will be glad to have brought a few snacks to fight the hunger pangs.
- Hospital towels are usually thin and scratchy, which is not what your partner wants to use for her first shower as a mom. Bring a nice fluffy pillow for her hospital bed as well and a neck brace for all the hours you might spend waiting on the bedside chair or out in the waiting room.

- Baby clothes, preferably in a few sizes, are also very important.
- Especially if you want to share the special moments from your baby's birth with your friends and family, a phone charger is very important.
- You can also bring a book, a laptop, or iPad for some pre and post-baby entertainment for you and your partner.

Active Labor

Active labor is the stage at which the baby starts trying to come out in real earnest. All the symptoms point to a rapidly exiting fetus pushing its way out of the cervix.

Contractions

As the cervix continues opening up with the contractions your partner is feeling, it is time to load up the car and take your partner to the hospital. By this time, she will be experiencing contractions every five minutes or so, with every one lasting more than a minute. The shortening and expanding of the cervix is what allows the woman to expel the baby. At this time, your partner may be very impatient, may yell contradictory commands, or may completely block you out and refuse to talk to you.

If you are holding her hand, the pain from her vice-like grip will be the least pain either of you will be feeling. With active labor pains, a contraction every two or three minutes and lasting for about one minute means that your partner is experiencing pain like she has never felt it before. Over time, the contractions get closer together leading up to the moment of labor pains on the delivery table.

You can help her to lessen the pain by using deep breathing techniques, but don't take it personally if she snaps at you or cusses you out if it doesn't work. Most importantly, however, you must keep in mind that your partner's distress during labor depends on her level of anxiety and the quality of support she receives. It is very important that you be completely supportive of your partner during her contractions. Let her have peace of mind knowing that you are there for her and that you are taking care of everything.

The less she has to worry about during this time, the better she will handle the pain. And if she decides to dish out some of her pain by clamping down on your hands even more tightly, the least you can do is bear it without complaining.

Water breaks

Passing the water held in the amniotic sac (breaking the water) is usually the very last sign that the baby is truly ready to come out. The actual process of passing this fluid differs from woman to woman. While some women feel a gush unlike anything they have ever experienced before, others feel a light trickle that might be mistaken for leaking urine. Yet it is very important that the baby is born as soon as the water breaks, because the amniotic fluid that is passed out plays a huge role in the protection of both the baby and the mother from infection. In most cases, contractions speed up right after the water breaks, as the birth process transitions into the second stage.

The Delivery Room

While it is possible to go through the early and active labor phases outside the delivery room, the following parts of birthing require the facilities of a maternity room and the expertise of a medical professional.

Transition

As your partner transitions into the second stage, her cervix will open up to reach about ten centimeters. In the meantime, her contractions will be occurring every two minutes and last more than one minute at a time. This is usually the most painful part of labor because the contractions are occurring so frequently, but the cervix has not opened up enough to allow for the baby to start coming out.

With no time to rest and no sign of an end to her labor pains yet (the baby has not started coming out yet), your partner will probably become very overwhelmed, both physically and emotionally. The transition stage is one that is filled with exhaustion, frustrations, and anger. If your partner is likely to become hostile towards you, the transition stage will be the first time she does it. For example, she might resent your touch even when she appreciated it in the start.

The Second Stage

In the second stage, the cervix opens up enough for the baby to start moving through the birth canal with every contraction. This is the moment when your partner will be asked to start pushing, as every contraction occurs to aid in moving the baby along. Even though the contractions will be just as strong as in the transition stage, they will become more spread out, giving your woman some level of relief in the interim. At the same time, the intensity of the contractions will probably still make your partner irritable and hostile.

Give her gentle encouragements and motivate her, but look out for those bursts of frustrations when she doesn't want to be touched or talked to. If she wants to be left alone, give her all the space she needs. If she wants you glued to her side, then that is where you must be. If she alternates between the two, hover around out of sight until you are wanted again. And, of course, remember all the events so that you can tease her about it later on.

Third Stage

The intensity of contractions comes down after the baby is completely out, but they don't go away completely just yet. She will continue feeling contractions as the uterus pushes the afterbirth out.

This happens as soon as five minutes after delivery but no longer than fifteen minutes later.

Fourth Stage

With all the pain behind her now, your partner will probably be very eager to hold and nurse her baby. Her frustrations and irritability will quickly give way to joy and relief, mixed with the physical exhaustion of the ordeal. The sooner she can start nursing, the sooner she will establish a bond with the baby and start the healing process.

Delivery Room Etiquette

In the delivery room, you will have no option but to place your partner in the hands of a professional. But this does not mean that your role in the birthing process comes to an end as soon as your wife gets to the hospital. You can still continue being her hero with the nurses and the friends and family who may have come to lend their support. You should do this by:

Speaking up for her

Having spent the last nine months planning for this day and talking about it with her, no one understands your partner's feelings about her baby more than you. When she is too overwhelmed to speak out, you should not hesitate to speak up and be your partner's advocate.

Distract her

In the delivery room, your purpose as your partner's support should always be to alleviate her pain. Anything you can do to do this will be welcome, including distracting her with stories and jokes—but only if she is in a position to appreciate them.

Be her coach

You can also coach your partner on the two most important things she will have to do during labor, breathing exercises and pushing. As the doctor gives out every "push" order, you can coach her through it perfectly if you are standing by her side. This is the moment to hold her hand (or let her hold yours as tightly as she wants) and get her through the exertion until you are holding the baby in your arms.

Cut the umbilical cord

This is not necessarily a responsibility that many men undertake, but it can be very fulfilling for you as the only member of your small family that can perform it. If you would like to give that snip that severs your partner and your baby, you should totally do it! However, you should be sure to follow the nurse's instructions to the letter.

Daddy Duties

Finally, there comes the moment you have both been waiting for: the moment the nurse hands you your bundle of joy and forever changes your life. I mean, you will probably only hold your son/daughter for a few seconds before passing him/her on to your partner, but that does not mean that you cannot appreciate the gravity of that moment. From this moment on, you are a father. Your life will never be the same again anymore. You have thought about the impending changes and the massive responsibility you will be taking on in a few months, but now you can see the face that puts a stamp on this new reality.

Whether you first receive your baby from the nurse or from your partner, you might be confused on how to hold him/her, all swaddled in layers and layers of shawls. In this section, I will give you a quick walk through the guidelines you need to follow as you take your baby in your arms for the first time.

- First off, always pick up the baby with clean hands. Wash your hands and wipe off the excess water if you have to.
- Make sure that you are in a comfortable stance before picking up your baby. You should have your full mobility, whether standing or sitting.

- As you extend your hands to receive the baby, spread out your fingers.
- Place one hand under the bottom and hips and the other hand cradling the back and encasing the back of the head. This ensures that you are giving as much support as possible to the baby's entire body.
- When handing him/her to others, maintain the support on the head and neck as well as the bottom and only release the baby to the other person when you are sure that they have a good handle on the baby to avoid possibly dropping and hurting it.

Welcoming Your Miracle Into the World

Now, as your partner recovers, it falls upon you to handle the logistics of welcoming your baby into the world. You will need to spend the first few hours with your partner and your baby, but it falls upon you to field the calls and the texts from friends and family. Take those first few moments to bond with your infant son or daughter and your wife/girlfriend and be sure to take pictures to commemorate the moment.

While she's at the hospital, take care of those finishing touches and make sure the home's ready for the arrival of the new family member. If you are holding a party to welcome the baby to the house, it is 100% your job to get the food, the decorations, and take care of any last minute concerns. A party is a great time to introduce all your family and friends to your baby, as well as give them an opportunity to offer assistance with the baby's future care needs. Believe me, you are going to need all the help you can get.

As you do all this, do not forget to take some time to recover from the birth. Even though the adrenaline rush will keep you going at the hospital, all the exhaustion will come crashing down on you as soon as you get a moment of rest. Do whatever you need to recharge both mentally and physically, and note what that thing is, because you are going to need it a lot in the coming months.

Chapter 3:

How to Handle Essential

Baby Care

The first few months of caring for your baby will probably be very stressful, especially if you have never cared for one before. Having no idea what you are doing, you might feel very overwhelmed, even stressed. The greatest fear that men have when caring for infants is that they might hurt their progeny. And while your wife might receive brochures for breastfeeding and some other baby care needs, there are no handouts for dads freaked out about changing a diaper or bathing the baby. You will just have to learn on the job.

Before you learn all these essential skills, you will probably find taking care of your baby tedious and nerve-racking. But as soon as you master these basic skills, you will find that taking care of your child becomes so much more enjoyable and you can even start bonding better. In this chapter, I will take you through some of the most important processes and skills you will need to develop. We will look at the best practices for comforting a baby, dressing them, changing diapers, getting a baby to fall asleep, feeding a baby, and dealing with irritableness from colic and teething, etc.

And at all times, make sure that you observe the supreme rule for baby care—make sure that the baby is comfortable at all times. Being unable to talk about their needs, your baby will use a very distressing signal to indicate their discomfort at every turn—crying. Your ability to deduce their needs from their cry will be directly proportional to your ability to care for him/her.

Changing a Diaper

Newborn babies are usually pooping and peeing machines, producing surprisingly massive amounts of waste. In fact, a baby usually needs to have his/her diaper changed every two hours on average. Of course, this frequency drops as the baby grows older, but for the time when you will need to make twelve diaper changes in one day, you have really got to be on top of your game. Failure to change a diaper in time can give your baby a terrible rash, whether her diaper has been soiled by poop or pee.

At the same time, you don't want to do a bad job of changing the diaper and leave the baby feeling uncomfortable or stinking all over the place.

Step-By-Step Guide to Changing a Diaper

1. Assess

What kind of damage are we talking about here, and what supplies will be necessary to deal with it? Also, where is the best place to perform this operation?

2. Secure the baby

After discovering that your baby has soiled his/her diaper, the first thing to do is move the baby to the changing table. If you don't have a specialized changing table, place a thick, non-permeable blanket underneath the baby to avoid smearing your couch or bed. You also need to make sure that the baby can't roll or fall off the changing surface. Obviously, this won't be a concern as you first learn your craft—newborns don't move anywhere—but as your child quickly matures, you will have to be highly vigilant. Don't doubt the warnings that tell you not to leave your child unattended.

3. Supplies

Have your supplies and keep them close. You don't want to hunt for butt cream when your squirming little one is already on the changing table, three feet above your hardwood floor. This is one benefit of having a changing station in your home. Your necessary supplies include a clean diaper, about five baby wipes, and baby powder. Keep them all close at hand as you start changing. If the waste has already leaked out of the diaper and soiled the clothes as well, get a new set to change the baby into before you put the baby in position for the change.

4. Precautions

Babies produce surprisingly stinky feces, especially when they are fed with formula. But even with breast milk, you should expect to be hit with a smell quite unlike any that you have experienced before. You can hold your breath till you have cleaned up the poop or simply put on a mask. No one will judge you— probably. Another very important precaution is to mind any incoming waste. It is quite common for babies to pee when they are naked. If you are positioned in the wrong way, you might find yourself needing to clean up and change.

5. Getting down to it

To get good access, lift the baby's lower body with one hand by gently hoisting him/her by the ankles. Remove the diaper and use the unsoiled parts to wipe everything clean down there. Take a fresh wipe and wipe any remaining waste in a front to back motion. The direction you take all the waste is important, because it reduces the amount of bacteria you are depositing on their more sensitive private parts, especially for girls.

6. Dispose of the soiled diaper

Place the used wipes inside the soiled diaper, bring the flaps down and make a bundle with the sticky parts for binding and throw it into the (preferably airtight) diaper bin.

7. Powder

A diaper can grow very hot for the baby. Adding the moisture and toxicity of the waste, you have the perfect conditions for a rash-filled baby bottom. To reduce the chances of this happening, apply a nice and even layer of powder on his/her bottom before putting another diaper on.

8. Fresh diaper

You should lay your baby down on the sticky tabs. Pulling them together just tight enough to keep the diaper secured to the legs doesn't make them too tight, as this tends to reduce circulation to the legs. If the diaper has a ruffle around the leg, leave it sticking out to ensure that there is no leakage once your baby soils this particular diaper.

Bath Time

Bathing a baby can be a very fun activity, but the first few days will probably not be part of this fun. The first bath your baby gets will have to be very well thought-out. In the first few days, your baby will be covered in a layer of protective wax called vernix. It keeps him/her safe from germs and other infectious stuff in the environment.

Moreover, for the first few days, and with the umbilical cord still attached, it would be very unsafe to bathe your baby by immersion. The navel requires the least possible amount of pressure in these first few days. Instead, you should use a soft sponge to clean the essentials, such as the head, hands, and diaper area. Only after s/he is a little older will it be safe to immerse your baby in a bathtub and give a thorough (but gentle) wash-over. However, even then you will not need to clean the baby every day. The only dirt he is picking up is his own waste, such as sweat and piss. You will only need to clean him/her once every few days for the first few months.

Giving a Sponge Bath

A sponge bath is the only approved way of cleaning your baby in those first few weeks when she/he is still very delicate and still shedding the umbilical cord, etc. It is also the washing style of last resort when you need to clean the baby without getting him/her completely drenched in the future.

Supplies

- You will need to have a towel or blanket to create a soft nest for your baby.
- The water you will use to wash the baby must be warm, not hot, to avoid scalding him/her. Ideally, the temperature should be just a degree or two above body temperature. The 98-99° F range is the recommended ideal temperature.
- Keep the washcloth with which you are to do the bathing close too. Be sure to use only the softest material possible to avoid irritating your baby's skin.
- Don't make the mistake of using *your* own soap to clean your baby. It will be too strong and might leave the baby's skin dry. Baby soaps are usually a lot milder and kinder on their soft skin and this is the only one that you should use.
- After cleaning, you must change the baby and put him/her in a fresh diaper and clothes. Keep them all close as well.

- Finally, you will need a baby towel. Some of the best baby towels come with a hood to keep your baby's head dry as he/she dries off.

Process

1. First off, adjust the temperature of the bathing room to around 75° F.
2. Take off the baby's diaper and remove her/his clothes. Place the diaper in the diaper bin and the clothes in the hamper. Cover your baby in a towel.
3. It is very advisable that you get a changing table because placing your son/daughter on the floor every time you wash him/her is not very ideal. If you do have a changing table, ensure that it has a strap you can use to keep him/her in place to avoid an accident.
4. All through the bath, expose only the part of the body that you are washing at any particular time. Start with the face and the head, dipping the washing sponge in clean warm water (no soap) for this part. Gently but thoroughly clean the eyes, the ears, the chin, and the fold of the neck. These are usually the parts that sweat most on a baby's face.

5. Add soap to the water and soak the sponge. Wring the sponge to remove all excess water and use this to wash your baby. Pay special attention to the armpits and the genitals.

6. Wrap the baby in the drying towel and dry him/her off and then put a fresh diaper and clean clothes on.

7. Follow the instructions of the doctor to the letter pertaining to bath time for a circumcised boy. The most important thing here is to keep the penis dry for as long as it takes to heal. Avoid the genitals when washing, in this event.

A Bathtub Bath

A bathtub is a more fun way of bathing your child. When s/he is older, this will become a nice way of bonding and getting yourself drenched in her/his splashy antics. For now, however, you will only be getting smiles and feeble splashes.

You will need the same supplies as for when you are giving the baby a sponge bath. The only difference is that you will require a lot more water.

1. An adult-sized bathtub will be too large for your baby. If you can, get a specialized baby bath at

the nearest baby supply store. Either way, fill the bathtub up to about three inches of warm water and no more. You want your baby to be immersed but not submerged, even while lying face-up in the water.

2. Undress the baby and immediately dip him/her in the warm water. To do this safely, use the classic baby-holding technique of placing one hand on the head and the other on the bottom. The faster you can do this, the better it will be for avoiding getting him/her wet.

3. Inside the water, position your baby in such a way that the head will always be above the water at all times. NEVER leave the baby in the bathtub alone for any reason whatsoever.

4. Use your hands to splash the warm water over his/her whole body. This keeps them warm and also tickles a little bit, so you will probably get a lot of giggle for it, if not right away, then later on when the baby has grown a little.

5. As with a sponge bath, do not use soap on the face. You can, however, wash his/her head with shampoo once or twice a week. Use the lightest touch in doing this to avoid any possibilities of hurting the baby's tender scalp. Also, use a different water bath with this to avoid mixing shampoo with the normal bathing water and soap.

6. For the rest of the body, dip a washcloth in the warm water and gently wash all the important parts (armpits, genitals, etc.)

7. Take your baby out of the bathtub and wrap him/her in a towel. As soon as this towel has absorbed all the water from the baby's skin, wrap him/her in a new dry one for warmth.

8. Proceed to dress the baby in a fresh diaper and clean clothes.

Master the bath

However slow you are to learn how to bathe your baby, you should always remember to:

1. Use a sink insert or special baby sink to wash the baby.

2. Only bathe the baby using his/her special baby soap.

3. Keep the water in the 98-99° F range. Use a bath thermometer to ensure that you get it just right. Another way you can check is by using the elbow or wrist, as these parts are more sensitive to temperatures.

4. Wash the baby only about four times a week, at most, in the first year. When baby starts moving around and touching everything, you might have to wash as much as twice a day.

5.   NEVER leave the baby alone in the bathtub.

Dressing the Baby

Unless you start doing it immediately after the baby arrives, which means that you learn *how* to do it early on, dressing the baby could turn out to be a lot harder than it seems. For one thing, babies don't much like being covered in layers and layers of clothes. Most babies tend to fight off any items of clothing you try to put on them. For another thing, there are rules to dressing a child. In this section, I will take you through the process in as much detail as possible. In the end, you should be able to dress up your baby just as well as any other person (read, your partner).

The Basics

The onesie

The onesie is the ultimate article of baby clothing. It covers the most important parts of your girl's/boy's body without inconveniencing the baby or you. For one thing, you only need to undo the snap buttons on the bottom to change the diaper. And since the hardest part of dressing a baby is getting his/her hands inside the sleeves, you will avoid fighting those tiny hands every time you change the diaper. As we have seen before, you will be doing this *a lot*.

The wrap shirt is another article of baby clothing that comes in very handy. Unlike the typical top, the wrap shirt has buttons all down the front so you don't have to pull it over the head – some babies dislike this aspect of dressing the most. Some wrap shirts have leggings too, which negates the need for a separate article of clothing. Whenever you need to change your baby, all you need to do is undo the buttons, remove the legs, handle your business, and get the legs back in.

Footwear

Babies don't really need to wear separate shoes or socks for the first few months because they don't really use their legs much. As such, you can just get the basic clothes like the wrap shirt or onesie with built-in socks.

Layers

Even if it is not cold, it is recommended that you keep your baby's whole body covered even if you only use light clothing. This will prevent accidental scrapes from hurting your tot's delicate skin. In the colder seasons or when you are going out, you might need to add a few more layers of thicker clothes to your baby's basic coverings. The general rule to protect from the cold is if you put on two layers of clothes for an outing, add an extra one for the baby. However, be careful not to add so many layers as to make him/her uncomfortable. If s/he is fussy, has flushed cheeks, or is sweating inside the clothes, then you should consider taking off a layer.

Accessories

When you start out, you may want to stick to the basic babywear like the onesie or wrap shirt. However, you can take it upon yourself to learn how to use accessories like skull caps, mittens, socks, and leg warmers as you go along. None of these accessories are ever decorative! The skull cap helps the baby maintain their body temperature by avoiding temperature loss through the head. Mittens are important to keep the baby from hurting themselves by scratching on their skin. In the event that you have dressed your baby in sockless clothes, socks will keep the feet warm. Leg warmers perform the same function (retaining heat) as socks.

A blanket covering

Special toddler blankets are important for keeping germs away, especially in the first few weeks and months when your baby's immune system isn't too strong. The blanket comes in handy during nursing, so don't forget it if you and your partner are going for an outing. Learn how to cover your tot's whole body except for the face. Be extra careful when handling your baby when s/he is covered in a blanket to prevent an accidental drop.

Special occasions

The car seat: Strapping your baby into the car seat will be extra complicated in the colder seasons because you want to keep her/him secure while also protecting from the cold. Remove any puffy clothes which might be dangerous in an emergency braking or impact situation, and use a blanket to wrap over the straps instead.

Sleep clothes: The less the clothes your baby is wearing during sleep, the safer s/he will be. Strictly keep away hats, mittens, and socks. They pose a serious hazard to your baby's well-being. Stick to a onesie and go for built-in accessories if you need to keep your tot from scratching her pretty little face.

Rules to Dressing a Baby

1. It is more about common sense and keeping your baby safe than fashion sense. You can forget matching the different articles of clothing for now, at least until you master the basics.
2. If possible, stick to snaps for undergarments. Zippers may snag on the skin and injure the baby, and buttons pose a choking hazard.
3. When opening or snapping the buttons shut, be careful not to press down onto the baby's body or pull on the clothes. Use both hands in any

dressing operations and place a finger underneath the snap when closing.

4. Never dress the baby in brand new clothes without first washing them. Chemicals used in the manufacturing and dying process might be harmful to the baby's skin. Be sure to throw any new clothes into the washer first.

Feeding Time

Feeding the baby is critical to his/her continued good health. The way the feeding happens, however, is mostly the prerogative of the mother. Let your partner decide whether she wants to breastfeed or use a bottle and do everything you can to help her either way.

Breastfeeding

If your partner decides to breastfeed, your role will be exclusively to offer her the support she needs during these moments. You can do this by:

Lending support any way you can

Breastfeeding can be a very painful and extremely stressful time for a new mother. Even if the baby is good at sucking, she might be hurting your partner's nipples with every milliliter of breast milk she suckles. But just because your baby can suck does not mean that she will be good at it. Some babies have trouble latching on, which can be a problem because doing so is the only way for them to become well-fed. Problems with latching on quickly become frustrating for both hungry babies and tired mamas.

If your partner is having trouble breastfeeding, embrace this problem as part of your parenting responsibilities. With good research, you can come up with different solutions, like fake nipples, to help out. If it turns out that you need to see a professional or try an alternative method of feeding the baby, be right by her side through the journey. However, limit your interference (if any at all) to the most distressing situations when your partner is at a loss. Your partner understands the phenomenon of breastfeeding better than you, so let her take the lead.

Being her butler

For as long as your partner is breastfeeding, she will be incapable of movement. Anything that is not within her reach will become useless to her, no matter how much she might need it. Moreover, she will not be able to perform any chores. The best way to contribute is by taking care of these small things and making her feel comfortable enough to take the time she needs to focus on feeding the baby. Bring her everything she needs to breastfeed, including snacks, if she needs, to replenish her energy while the baby feeds.

Helping with the pumping

If your partner decides to pump her milk instead of feeding the baby directly from the teat for whatever reason, you can help out there too. The process of pumping can be just as time-consuming as breastfeeding. Lend a hand to give her the peace of mind to do this without stressing about much else. You can also help in cleaning the pumps. To do this, follow this strict regimen recommended by the CDC:

1. Clean your hands with soap and water beforehand and keep them clean throughout the process.
2. Take the pump apart and clean every part individually, starting with a rinse with running water.
3. Use a specialized basin and scrub to clean your pump.
4. After cleaning, rinse the parts in clean water in a fresh new basin.
5. Let the cleaned parts and the cleaning equipment air dry. Don't use a towel to dry, as it increases the possibilities of spreading germs.

6. When cleaning with a dishwasher, use hot water and the heated drying mechanism. Even better, use the "sanitize" setting.

7. You can assemble the pump before storing or keep the individual parts separate afterwards, but be sure to store them in a clean and dry place. You can buy special containers for this purpose; just be sure to keep them thoroughly sterilized and dry before using them for storage.

Burping the baby after feeding

Burping allows the baby to let go of any gas that may have been ingested along with the milk. When these bubbles remain inside the stomach, they will make your baby uncomfortable. By burping effectively after every feeding, you can eliminate stomach gas from the possible causes of discomfort any time your baby starts to cry.

Burping occurs when you pat or rub the baby's back softly. For the most effective burping, you should place the baby on your shoulder or on your lap. Be sure to place a burping cloth over whatever you are wearing to avoid soiling your clothes.

Bottle Feeding

There are quite a number of reasons to choose to feed the baby using a bottle rather than directly from the breasts. First off, s/he could be having trouble latching on, or your partner simply prefers the less stressful (and less painful) method of bottle feeding. Or she could be having trouble producing sufficient milk for the baby, in which case you will have to resort to baby formula, either to supplement the breast milk mom pumps or for all your feeding needs.

Either way, feeding the baby through a bottle is considerably less stressful compared to breastfeeding. It also presents you with an opportunity to help your partner in the actual feeding of the baby. But if your partner is pumping milk and feeding the baby through a bottle, this will be an extra task for her after going through the pumping ordeal. You should help out by:

Taking on the job of sterilizing the bottles

Hygiene is of utmost importance when it comes to feeding the baby. The bottles need to be sterilized and the pumps need cleaning before and after every use. This is a simple job that you can do with relative ease.

1. Start with cleaning your hands thoroughly.

2. Inspect the feeding bottles and throw out any bottles or teats with cracks. They usually act as a breeding ground for bacteria and harmful germs.

3. Depending on the method of sterilization you are using, the third step differs.

   i. If you are using water, simply put everything into hot water and use soap to clean everything up. Pay special attention to the small parts, such as screw areas and the suckling hole.

   ii. If you are using a steam sterilizer, you simply need to add water and turn the machine on.

   iii. If you are using the microwave, put the bottle and teats inside and turn it on at the right temperature.

   iv. With the boiling method, put the feeding supplies in a pot and fill it with water.

4. When the feeding equipment is all cleaned, remove them (use tongs if they are too hot) and place them in the sterilized storage container.

Helping select the right formula

Sometimes the baby does not take on well to the formula you have him on. Help your partner to find the formula that is best suited to your baby. If your baby has trouble with the first one you try, consult your pediatrician before trying anything new.

Preparing the formula

Hygiene is of utmost importance when feeding the baby. Everything you use in preparing the baby formula should be specially washed and sterilized for that purpose only.

1. Boil a quart of fresh tap water and let it cool to about 160° F. This should take about thirty minutes.
2. Disinfect the table or countertop where you prepare the formula.
3. Wash your hands with soap and lots of water.
4. Place the bottle on the cleaned countertop and pour the exact amount of water you need to make the formula.
5. Scoop out the recommended amount of formula for the water you have in your feeding bottle and add to the water in the bottle.

6. Without touching inside or on the parts that will screw onto the feeding bottle, screw it onto the bottle and cover it with the cap.

7. Give the bottle a gentle shake until the formula dissolves in the water to form a consistent mix.

8. Cool the formula to bring it down to the ideal temperature for the baby. This is at exactly body temperature as felt at the back of your hand.

9. When feeding, you can let the baby dictate how much of the formula s/he takes. Sometimes the baby will go to sleep on the bottle and wake up needing more, and sometimes s/he just stops feeding.

10. Throw away any leftover formula and NEVER reuse it.

Waking up to feed the baby at night too

So maybe you need to be up early for work tomorrow and it is impossible to wake up in the middle of the night to feed the baby. This does not mean that you cannot help out. You can take over feeding and baby care to give your partner a head start on sleep before you get to bed yourself. Or you can wake up early the next morning and give the baby his/her first bottle.

Sleep Time

Watching your baby sleep will be one of the most satisfying moments of parenting you will ever enjoy. At the same time, dealing with your baby when s/he is stubbornly refusing to sleep or nap will be one of the most stressful parts of parenting. In the early months, your baby will be sleeping as much as 16 hours a day, only s/he will be doing it in chunks of two to four hours at a time. The baby will demand attention and require feeding and changing in the time he is awake, so you cannot leave him/her alone. In this section, I will give you a few tips that you can follow to handle your baby's sleeping patterns better.

Create a Schedule

The intermittent sleeping patterns of your tot will create a huge problem for parents because they can never get enough sleep all at once unless they get help. However, you can tackle this problem using creativity, by breaking up the night into early and late shifts. While your partner sleeps, you take care of the baby and vice versa. Any additional help you can get from friends or family would also help in a huge way.

Bedtime Routine

A bedtime routine allows you to modify the baby's sleeping time and even induce sleep. Even if the baby is still too young to be going the whole night without waking up, you can help him/her sleep better (and longer) by establishing a schedule for the main snooze of the day. The simpler the routine, the easier it will be to maintain.

Teach the Baby to Self-Soothe

If you wait until the baby is asleep in your arms before putting her/him in the crib, she will never learn to go to sleep on her own. Instead, you should learn to spot the drooping eyes of a drowsy child and put her/him in the crib at this point. The more your baby learns to go to sleep on her/his own, the more peaceful a sleeper s/he will become.

This is called self-soothing and it basically teaches the baby to put him/herself to sleep. Later on, when s/he can sleep for longer, you will be extra thankful when your baby awakens and then puts herself back to sleep. If you do not teach your baby to self-soothe, you might still be dealing with sleeping problems when the baby is three years old!

Understand Your Baby's Needs

The first rule to mastering your baby's sleep time is learning to read his/her body language. When he is sleepy, the baby will rub his eyes, yawn, or become extra fussy. This is the point at which you put him through the bedtime routine and put him to sleep.

Dealing With Fussiness

Your baby will not sleep if she is experiencing any discomfort. And even if she does, it will not last long before you awaken to baby's cries once again. So, if the baby is fussy before you put her to bed, you can check a few things to calm her down enough to go to sleep.

Check for Pain

A baby in pain will cry for hours on end and have trouble settling down long enough to go to sleep. You need to learn to check for any sources of discomfort in your baby and (of course) how to correct them.

Swaddling

If the baby is sleepy but is having trouble actually falling asleep, you should consider swaddling as the solution. A swaddle helps the baby sleep better by keeping their arms and legs from flailing around too much. The swaddle also helps to soothe an overstimulated baby and reduces the levels of fussiness s/he exhibits. Just be careful not to swaddle too, tightly as this might affect the baby's mobility development.

Some Essentials

In this section, I will highlight some of the most important baby care concerns that you might have as a dad.

Putting Your Baby in the Crib

- The only correct position is with the baby on her/his back.
- Always have the baby sleep in the crib, but keep it in your room.

- The crib must be safety approved and contain no objects like toys or pillows that might pose a danger to the baby.
- Do not overdress the baby. A single layer of clothes is enough to ensure maximum comfort. For extra warmth, use a swaddle or a wearable blanket.
- Use the same temperature setting as you would if the baby was not in the room with you.

Putting Your Baby in the Stroller

The baby will need a different kind of stroller at different ages, but it is all about the mechanics when it comes to this very important accessory. As the dad, you are 100% in charge of buying the right stroller for your baby. Things to look out for include:

- **A low center of gravity:** This will help to avoid tipping, especially when the baby is old enough to move around.
- **Adjustable seat:** Sometimes your baby will be very keen to watch the scenery. At other times s/he will be rocked to sleep by the motion of the stroller. With an adjustable seat, your baby will be able to do both of these things very comfortably.

- **Reliable brakes:** You want a stroller that allows you to lock the wheels effectively whenever you need to, without disengaging and rolling away without you.
- **The weight:** If you will be traveling with the stroller, you will have to load it into the car and unload it when you reach your destination. The same goes for your partner as well. Get a stroller that doesn't make every small journey a weightlifting competition.

As for putting the baby into the stroller, the guidelines are the same for placing him/her into the car seat as we discussed before. Even though there is less risk of impact with a stroller, you want your baby to be snugly strapped into the seat.

Checking for Discomfort

Even though they don't express them verbally, babies feel a wide range of emotions. Typically, positive emotions will be expressed with a toothless smile that melts your heart, and any discomfort will be expressed through crying. The problem is that there is no explicit way of knowing what the baby is crying about. Your parenting experience is what will give you a clue as to the reason. Maybe she's hungry, or her diaper is full and it's irritating her bottom. Usually, s/he will quiet down as soon as you fix the problem.

But then there are those cries caused by discomfort. They are a little harder to figure out. However, knowing that your baby is crying from discomfort and not hunger will help you in figuring out exactly what might be causing the crying. So how do you differentiate between a discomfort cry and other types of cries? Well, for one thing, the cry will be more high-pitched and unrelenting. The facial expressions will also be more distressed and the posture stiff and fidgety.

- When colic is the cause of discomfort, the baby will tend to arch his back as he cries, thrash the legs and the arms around, and keep the fists tightly clenched.
- Teething is another huge cause of discomfort in babies. It is accompanied by drooling and sucking on fingers.
- Discomfort from a stomach upset will usually be indicated by cries accompanied by squirming.

Even as you plan to take your baby to the pediatrician to have him/her checked out, keep in mind that you are the first line of defense. Touch the baby, massage, and sing to him/her. Not only does this soothe the pain response areas of your baby's brain, it also soothes you and helps to keep you from freaking out completely.

Another important secret is to learn to follow your instincts. The bond between your baby and you is a lot stronger than you might think—especially if you have been working on it. Trust in yourself to figure out what is wrong and help your baby cope.

Chapter 4:

Your Emotional Well-being

in a Post-Pregnancy World

In much of the fatherhood literature out there, you will hardly find a mention of the feelings that new dads go through. These authors, well-meaning as they are, focus solely on the nitty-gritty of taking care of the baby. They forget that dads need caring for as well, or they won't be able to take care of the baby. I mean, how do you deal with the uncertainty, the isolation, and the jealousy? You will feel rotten for missing—or even wishing for—the good old days when you and your partner had just each other.

In the worst-case scenario, you will also have difficulty bonding with your child for the first few months. Engrossed with motherhood, your partner will most likely be too preoccupied with the baby to notice any of what you will be going through. In this chapter, we will examine the common emotions you can expect to feel after the baby's birth as well as the relationship changes likely to occur as a result of your bundle of joy's coming into your life.

Emotions You Can Expect to Feel

Like motherhood, fatherhood is a rollercoaster of emotions that only those who have been through it can appreciate. The most challenging thing about parenthood is the expectations that people feel to act in particular ways. You feel the pressure very deeply when everyone around you just expects you to feel happy and excited all the time. This is especially the case when people judge you for having feelings different from others in a similar position. So, you lock your real feelings deep down and put on a brave face. But how effective is that? I suggest that you take a different approach. Recognize all these emotions early on, figure out what your heart is trying to tell you, and use this to improve yourself as a father.

Excitement—but Also Helplessness

Fatherhood is exciting. It gives you an opportunity to become a full family. You have probably developed a pretty comprehensive idea of the kind of dad you would like to be already, and it is time to realize your dream. How exciting is that? At the same time, what if you fail? What if you end up being a terrible father and giving your daughter/son serious daddy issues? What if you become the reason your child struggles to form relationships later on in life?

This helplessness works very much like a curtain falling in front of all the excitement you are feeling about fatherhood and blocking all the joy off. The truth is, you cannot control how the future of your newborn child plays out. You cannot protect him/her from the falls, the heartbreaks, and other adversities s/he will encounter along the way. Before you accept this fact, you will struggle with the helplessness of your situation. Loving your child so much yet knowing that there is little you can do to protect them from the world around them will be hard.

To alleviate your feelings of helplessness, you can start by helping around the house and doing everything you can to become the caring dad for your son/daughter. Only by fostering a strong bond with your baby will you get the opportunity to be super dad and protect your child from any threats around them.

Joy—but Also Guilt

Any moments you spend bonding with your baby or supporting your partner as she handles the complicated baby care operations, like learning to breastfeed, will bring you a lot of joy. If you are bottle-feeding the baby, you will also experience the joy of feeding the baby in a huge way. It is tempting for new parents to get trapped in the baby vortex and only feel good when caring for him/her. This is especially the case when there are some challenges in the process. Knowing that you are doing everything you can to make life easier for your family just feels right.

Until you feel neglected and decide to indulge yourself a little. For example, you may decide to catch a quick game or go out for a jog to clear your head. You know, the things that bring you joy and make you appreciate life. The truth is that if you are a jogger or if you enjoy football, it forms a part of your identity. It gives you the emotional and physical energy you need to care for your baby. But the indulgence will cost you a measure of guilt. In fact, any personal time you take as a new parent comes with a lot of guilt.

Any time you feel guilty for indulging in personal pleasures, just remember that you are only as good a father as the person you are. And if you are grouchy and high-strung because you don't get to indulge in your personal pleasures anymore, you will only grow to resent the baby. I am not saying don't make sacrifices— you will definitely need to make a few. However, I would not advise giving up anything that contributes to your overall well-being.

An Outpouring of Childhood Emotions

You would think that bringing a child into the world is an opportunity for the parent to look into the future, but studies indicate that most parents experience a more backwards turn. According to attachment theoreticians, we see parenting as an opportunity to relive our own childhood—our way. For people with childhood traumas or repressed emotions from the earliest phase of their lives, parenthood can be very unsettling. If you have not had an opportunity to come to terms with your childhood, then you are in the twilight period of your innocence. In a few months, you will be welcoming your baby into the world—and coming face to face with your own childhood.

It is very important that you come to terms with your childhood emotions and create harmony in that area of your life. Because whether you like it or not, your childhood does play a part in the kind of parent you would like to be. This is even more important if you faced some traumas as a child or as a teenager.

But even if your childhood was innocent and carefree, there are some very nuanced influences that might affect your ability to parent. For example;

- If you were treated harshly after getting upset, you may have internalized that distress is an emergency which would send you into fight or flight mode. The problem with this is that your child will become the enemy any time his/her actions upset you.

- Children can be very perceptive about respect (or lack thereof) in their interactions with adults. If your parents did not treat you with due respect, you might unwittingly transfer this over to your child.
- Critical parents often raise perfectionist children, who grow up into perfectionist adults. Perfectionist adults become perfectionist parents who criticize their children and impose very high, often unachievable standards. On the flip side, perfectionist parents make their children feel like they need to *earn* their love, which can be very unsettling.

Here is the rather unsettling thing about childhood issues—they come out no matter how well your parents raised you. Unless you put in the work of figuring out your emotions, you will remain unaware of those triggers that might affect your ability to parent well. Now is the time to get ahead of these triggers and ensure that you are at peace with your childhood, before it is too late.

A Deeper Connection to Your Partner—but Also Emotional Distance

For some couples, welcoming a baby into the relationship strengthens the bond between you and makes you closer than ever before. There are times when everything just falls into place, you feel even closer to your partner, and life looks bright. This, of course, is the perfect-case scenario. The reality is often a lot less cheery.

Babies have a way of grabbing the spotlight and never letting go. From the moment she arrives, the baby will demand most (if not all) of your and your partner's attention. With the constant crying, late nights, and disrupted sleep patterns, it is very likely that you and your partner will grow somewhat distant immediately after the birth.

Paternal Postpartum Depression

In some cases, the joy of fatherhood is quickly replaced by unrelenting fear and anxiety, which soon blossoms into full-blown depression. This is called Paternal Postpartum Depression (PPPD), not to be confused with maternal postpartum depression, although there have been extensive studies showing a sizable correlation. Men with partners going through maternal postpartum depression are as much as 50% more susceptible to getting PPPD. If getting depression following your daughter's/son's birth sounds tragic, that is because it is. Fathers going through PPPD tend to fixate on problems, blow them out of proportion, and may even lash out.

The last thing anyone in your household needs is to be dealing with a full-grown man throwing tantrums or drinking right now. You know you are supposed to be the protector and the provider, but how are you supposed to handle *this* particular issue? DO NOT let the old-school notions of the invincible man twist your thinking. Failing to get help is the assured way of harming your family. You need to get help.

You should visit a therapist if you are exhibiting the following signs:

- You quarrel and get angry with others a lot more frequently.
- You are using alcohol and street drugs as a coping mechanism to deal with your stress.
- You are irritable and frustrated, especially when there is no apparent cause for your irritability.
- You feel pent-up and exhibit signs of violent behavior.
- You gain a significant amount of weight or you lose a good amount of it.
- You feel increasingly isolated from your friends and family, especially your wife and child.
- You get stressed easily and have trouble shaking off the stress once it takes root.

- You engage in impulsive behaviors and take unnecessary risks, such as having an affair or driving dangerously.
- You have the feeling that nothing will ever be good again. You are discouraged.
- You experience constant headaches, indigestion, and body aches.
- You are unmotivated and have trouble concentrating on any given task.
- You lose interest in things that previously gave you pleasure such as sex, your hobbies, or work.
- You use work as a shield between you and the world and between you and your family.
- Even while you spend all your time at the office (work), you are not as productive as you should be.
- You feel that you are not the kind of man you would like to be. You are disappointed in yourself.
- You are entertaining thoughts about death and suicide.

Postpartum depression may develop as a result of a difficult adjustment to having a baby in your life. In the event that you are part of the 50% of men who get PPPD along with their partners, you are in an even more precarious situation. You need to get help as soon as possible to ensure the continued safety of your child.

Why It Happens

Essentially, PPPD is happening because the role of fatherhood is changing. The expectations that men and society have about male parenting have experienced a seismic shift in the last few decades. We are now asking of ourselves things that our ancestors would never have dreamed of. The fear and anxiety that causes PPPD indicates the lack of preparedness that men have for their changing fatherhood roles. If you are taking turns waking up to comfort the baby in the middle of the night, the lack of sufficient sleep increases your chances of anxiety.

Then there are the additional pressures that men feel, such as the financial stress of caring for a new member of the family, balancing work (and your old life) with caregiving, and lower levels of testosterone. All these factors play a part in opening men up to emotional and mental discord much like it does with mothers.

How to Deal With It

Dealing with PPPD requires a comprehensive approach entailing:

Overcoming the stigma

You probably feel the need to be strong and capable a lot more strongly now that you are a father, which is why you will find it rather difficult to own up to your postpartum depression. But here's the thing—you are not the only one! Men suffer from depressive mood disorders all the time; it is just that they don't go announcing it. And if you really want to become strong, then be strong for your family. Admit that you need help to harness your fears and anxieties and channel them productively, and go get that help!

Seeking professional help

The good thing about treatments for PPPD is that they tend to be short and effective. For example, cognitive behavior therapy gives you the tools you need to understand how your emotions affect your behavior. It takes an average of three months to complete. Other therapies like relationship management improve self-worth and give you the tools you need to build the quality of your relationships. In general, therapy gives you power and makes you feel more in control of your own thoughts and feelings.

Reaching out

Sometimes you develop depressive symptoms because you get too much into your own head. You start judging yourself (harshly, of course) and you fall short of your own expectations. You can get a better perspective on your merit as a father by talking to other fathers and sharing your frustrations and your fears. Talk to people who are already dads—your own father, a co-worker, a stranger at the park—and get their perspectives. You might be surprised to find that you have always been a pretty good dad. And if nothing else, this will take some of the pressure off.

P.S.

I cannot reiterate this enough: caring for your family starts with caring for yourself. Self-care is the ultimate remedy to postpartum depression. And this goes for you and your partner as well. It is no good (especially for the baby) if you give up your pleasure pursuits only to have your well-being take a dip.

Your Relationship After Baby's Arrival

Relationships tend to change as soon as the baby arrives, and usually not for the better. Some couples accept less intimacy as part of becoming new parents, but this is not how it is meant to be. And even though your relationship will definitely change after the birth of a child, you can do something about it. In this section, we will touch on some common relationship issues and ways that you can handle them.

Common Relationship Issues

As soon as the baby arrives, you discover that there are too many things that need to be done. Even worse, there will always be something to do at any given time. This limits your freedom to indulge both as a person and as a couple.

In some cases, fathers have to fight to get their partners to accept their views on how to take care of the baby. It is a no-win situation whereby you feel like a jerk if you contradict your wife. After all, she did carry the baby for nine months and suffer the pains of breastfeeding, etc. When you don't voice your views, you become resentful and the relationship suffers.

As a couple, you are either sleeping late and waking up early or sleeping early and waking up super early or multiple times in the night. One or both of you will be suffering from sleep deprivation, making you snappy and reactive—not exactly the recipe for a happy couple.

Like it or not, sex plays a huge part in fostering intimacy between any romantic couple. But with the crazy hours and never-ending baby care, you will hardly ever have time for it. Moreover, your partner will probably be feeling very unsexy in light of her recent bodily changes. It also can take weeks for a mother's body to heal after childbirth, which can make the experience of sex highly unpleasurable.

A relationship will only be as good as the people in it are feeling. At some point, the personal frustrations will come pouring out and sour everything. So, if you are not getting any "me" time, your entire relationship is very likely to suffer as well.

The extended family can be a huge blessing when they take over the duties of caring for the baby and giving you and your partner the chance to get some alone time, apart and together. At the same time, constantly having family around will make it harder to hit the levels of intimacy you are used to.

How to Handle These Problems

You can solve any relationship issues that crop up by simply talking about it in a calm and rational manner. It is better to have a fight about a contentious issue and get it out of the way than to have it bubble under the surface and poison your relationship in the shadows.

As her companion, your job is to look out for your partner. You should always keep in mind that your partner was affected by the birth and the immense changes in her body more than you. If you recognize the signs of postpartum depression, support her as she seeks help and be there for her along the way as well.

With a baby between you, you cannot just take a break from the relationship "to think things over." However, you can definitely take a timeout when things get too heated and unproductive. You can use the Lily and Marshall "pause" button from "How I Met Your Mother" to avoid escalating issues and to gain some perspective.

Your partner shutting down and going into "mommy" mode all the time will probably be the biggest hindrance you face as you try to revive the relationship flame. Sometimes all you need is to show her that you are in this together. You can do this by engaging in parenting tasks together. As you bond over the baby, you will find that it gets easier to talk her into scheduling 20 to 30 minutes per day for just the two of you to reconnect.

How to Strengthen Your Relationship After the Baby

Overcoming the issues that come up along the way is not nearly enough if you are in a loving, caring relationship. You need to find ways of using the baby to make you and your partner a stronger couple. After all, the stronger you are, the better you will be as parents.

Understand that you are a team

Most couples make the mistake of making baby care a competition or a game of one-upping each other. The small misgivings that competition brings add up, and not in anyone's favor.

Laugh together

The importance of laughter in a relationship cannot be overlooked. If you can laugh together, then you can love together. And if you can love together, nothing can get between you.

Embrace the predictability

The worst mistake you can make as a new parent is to keep clinging to the old ways when you made decisions on the fly. Accept the fact that, to a large extent, spontaneity will disappear from your life instead of trying to "live in the moment" and other such bachelor nonsense. Plan ahead for bonding moments and anything you want to do with your family.

Practice patience

Among the things that you will need to be patient about is your partner's infatuation with the baby. For the first couple of days, she will probably spend all her waking time in service to the baby. As the weeks roll by, she will keep cutting down until you can have your fair share of both her and the baby. Keep in mind that nothing is permanent and your situation (whatever it might be) will improve substantially in a few months.

Play your part

Baby care responsibilities are to be shared with your partner. In the first few days/weeks, your partner will probably take on every aspect of baby care. This is not an opening for you to abdicate. At some point, you will have to come in and handle a few things. The more the duties you are able to help out with, the better off you will both be as a team.

Chapter 5:

Working as a Team

The old saying "it takes a village to raise a child" is true for first-time parents. With your limited experience raising a child, any help will come in very handy. In fact, you might find yourself needing help a lot more than you ever anticipated. The more help you receive from friends and family, the easier the whole experience will be for both of you. In this chapter, we will discuss teamwork in raising a baby. Of course, the team of you and your partner will be the most important one in this process. But you cannot ignore the role of family, friends, and neighbors in your baby's growth. You will definitely get visitors bringing you supplies and plying you with (sometimes unsolicited) advice.

Among the many things you will have to decide about your baby, you should prepare to answer the question of how you plan to split up responsibilities with your partner. If there are grandparents, aunts, and uncles, they will be eager to put in their time caring for the baby as well. While many new parents struggle with scheduling after the birth, it's imperative for maintaining sanity and leading a productive life. As you bring a new addition to your nuclear family, you will also have to welcome the baby into your extended family.

Making Teamwork Work

Depending on your personality, you either find having people in your home energizing or extremely draining. But because baby care is not just about you, you will have to keep your partner's needs in consideration as well. The idea of having people around after the baby is born is one you will have to revisit over and over again in the next couple of months. Keep tweaking it until you find something that works for both of you. Of course, if you and your partner find other people draining and don't feel the need to have friends and family help out, you can find ways to cover everything yourselves. Hired help, for example, is one thing that you can control and a good assistant will not invade your lives.

However, even if you do not mind having help, you will still need to find a way to organize it into a coherent support system. The last thing you want is for your support system to degenerate into chaos. In this section, we will look at some of the best ways to welcome people into your baby's life without making yourself irrelevant.

Keep the Numbers Low

A small team of efficient and eager helpers will go farther than a large team of haphazard, half-hearted help. I am talking about the very core of your inner circle, parents, and siblings. These are the people who, first off, understand you best. They know if you are particular about the way things flow and they have a vested interest in taking care of your baby—granny, uncle, and auntie points. If you can count on a few trustworthy friends to give you a combined number of hours' help every day, then you and your partner can find the time to get enough sleep and get your lives back on track.

Communicate Your Vision Beforehand

As much as your closest friends are committing a few hours of their time to help you, you have to appreciate that they have their own lives as well. From the word go, you and your partner need to communicate with would-be helpers about the level of help you are willing to accept (or how much you will need). In the coming months, you will learn to value reliability over anything else. It is the people whom you can really count on 100% who will be most helpful.

Set Boundaries

If you need assistance and extended family members offer help, do accept. But set some conditions. The people who help you should help you to raise your daughter/son the way you want him/her raised. You should make that absolutely clear from the word go to avoid any confusion. You can also limit the activities that your team of helpers can do. For example, you can carve out activities like feeding, changing, and soothing for the support group and take it upon yourself to bathe and put the baby to sleep. Some issues like feeding can be very divisive, with the people for and against breastfeeding, for example, being very assertive in their views. As the husband, you have a huge role to play in beating off any opposition to you and your partner's preferred way of doing things. When you present a united front, you will get to raise your baby exactly as you want.

Carve out Family Time

Sometimes the help you get comes from very experienced caregivers like your mothers. And sometimes, the help they give you is not really help, but criticism and a complete takeover. Sometimes the help of authority figures like parents can be domineering, especially if you are not very assertive. You will appreciate all the time you spend with just your partner and your baby in the future.

Find a Way to Deal With Visitors

Some people show up unannounced, just to give their opinion and then disappear without doing much in the way of helping. Even if a visitor comes in for a few hours to help, you will not benefit much from it, because it is not something you control. We will discuss visitation policy in more detail below, but I need to make the point that visitors don't do much for you or your partner. Sometimes all your partner wants to do is take care of the baby or rest. If visitors are not the very helpful kind, then you ought to run interference for her.

Coordinate Home Stays

If you get paternity leave, it will not be enough to take your partner through the whole process of recovery and getting into the flow of raising a child. In cases of caesarean birth, your partner will be bedridden for weeks and unable to do much work for months afterwards. If you can get a few weeks of help from retired moms, aunties, or pretty much anyone who can make the time, take it. You can bring together all the people who are available to help and create a schedule that works for everyone.

Manage Egos

There could be a lot of hurt feelings between you and your helpers as well as between the helpers themselves. Competition might even break out and disrupt the balance you have over the whole thing. In-laws are especially given to power tussles that might turn an otherwise joyful experience into a stressful time for your whole family. You need to make everyone feel valued, but obviously you have to keep in mind that different people put in different levels of effort. Appreciating the help you receive is very important. Be sure to tell everyone on your team these things—in explicit terms—right to their faces.

Keep Your Priorities Right

At the end of the day, your job and the job of your team of helpers is to give your partner (the new mom) as smooth a transition as possible into her new role. This means that you need to make special considerations for her sake. For example, depending on how well she is handling the experience of being a new mother and the relationship with your own mother, it might be necessary to limit your family's involvement in the process, even if she gets her family to come and stay with her.

Dealing With Overzealous Involvement

Unless the involvement of friends and family is doing more harm than good, you should count yourself happy. The more others help, the less you have to do, and the more time you will have to spend with your family. However, when the help is disruptive, then you may have to put your foot down and set (and enforce) some guidelines. Limit the frequency and duration of visits to whatever works for you.

Dealing With Tepid Involvement

I bet you did not think about this happening, huh? Unfortunately, it happens quite frequently. Sometimes the people in your circle are too busy to make time to help out for hours at a time. It is just something that you will have to accept. If it bothers you, you can confront them and ask why. It could be that their perceptions about you and your partner as a self-sufficient couple are keeping them away. If not, then you might just have to find hired help and deal with your resentments later.

The Importance of Teamwork

Some new parents make the mistake of ignoring the responsibilities talk early on. This leads to strife and quarrels that might impair your ability to organize a united front as you tackle the complexities of baby care. You should have the discussion about responsibilities as early as possible instead of taking things that the other person does for granted.

Split Tasks Don't Seem So Daunting

When you think about all the laundry your baby is producing along with all the utensils, the hours needed to feed, burp, wash, and do other house chores, you might feel overwhelmed. This is especially so if your partner is still recovering from the birth. But if you get a couple of friends and/or relatives to help out every few days, then it all seems less overwhelming. Getting help allows you to deal with fewer tasks, which in turn allows you to dedicate more time to bonding with your son/daughter.

You Can Go Back to Work

If you are a working dad, the only way you can go back to work, especially if you need to do it soon after the baby is born, is with a team of helpers picking the slack back at home. It is not like you can just stop working, especially now that your family is getting bigger, so any help to that end will be highly appreciated. If you decide to organize helpers by shifts, take the last shift of the day or the first one in the morning to ensure that you also get to spend time with the baby.

On this point, a team plays an even bigger role in keeping your partner company during the day while you work. Knowing that there is always someone lending a helping hand in your absence will give you the peace of mind to focus on your work all through the day.

You Can Both Get Enough Sleep

With helpers (especially live-in helpers), you are in a great position to plan ahead, including for important aspects of your lives like sleep. This works best if you are bottle feeding. Your partner can just pump the milk and leave it with the nighttime helper, catching a full night of sleep and knowing that the baby is still well-fed.

Visitation Policy

It is common for you and your partner to feel overwhelmed—even exhausted—by visitors, and it is within your rights to decide to regulate the flow. With the very first news blast you send out announcing the arrival of your bundle of joy, you should let everyone know how you feel and determine when you're going to be ok with others visiting your home to meet the baby. In this section, we will look at the best visitation policies you can employ at different points in the parenting journey.

At the Hospital

As the only person allowed into the delivery room, you are in the best position to deal with well-wishers. While you and your partner are in the delivery room welcoming your baby into the world, you will probably have to step outside a few times to give updates on the progress.

You will have to develop a way of showing your appreciation for the support while giving your partner and yourself the time to bond with the baby. You get to step outside and announce, "it's a girl/boy!" and then request that they come in for the first look before announcing that it is time to try breastfeeding (or resting for the mother).

The important thing is that you manage the whole process exactly how your partner and you would wish it to go. Do not let visitors interfere with your opportunity to bond with and over the baby. If you decide that you want this experience to be yours alone, then that is exactly how it should be.

At Home

When you bring your partner and your baby home from the hospital, you are bringing them into the next chapter of all your lives—as a family. You should decide how you want to handle this transition, including the amount of privacy you would like to maintain. You can start this new chapter of your life with a small party, or you might take the first week alone with your tiny family. It is all up to you.

However, it is harder to keep visitors away from the house forever. At some point, you will need their help dealing with the extra chores and attending to the baby. But at the same time, you need to establish some ground rules.

No surprises

The worst thing you can put your partner through at this time is having to entertain a string of surprise visits when she would just like to spend the time bonding with the baby. Getting a heads-up allows you to prepare for what is coming and to enjoy the down times without worrying about the doorbell ringing with a surprise visitor.

Purpose matters

The best kind of visitor is the one who can come in and move around the house to take care of the things that you have been too busy to take care of such as grocery shopping, without bothering you too much. For example, someone who is always around the house and knows how you like things to be will be perfectly capable of coming in and working unsupervised. The other guests who call in to "check on" you tend to be more of a nuisance.

Similarly, you should not be ashamed to put visitors to work. For example, if you don't have someone helping out in the kitchen, you can ask people to bring food. The people who really care will be glad to help. Those who balk at helping out are of no use to you anyways. It is good that you learn that now.

Spacing

Having too many people crammed in your living room can be very tiresome. At some point, it will start feeling like you are in a boring party that never ends. The best kind of spacing is one where you schedule out chunks of time, such as nap time, as no-visit times. This is especially important because most visitors will want to hold the baby and comment about his/her nose, ears, and eyes.

Things have to go your way

To some extent, when it comes to entertaining visitors, it becomes sort of an "us" versus "them" situation. The "us" includes you, your partner, and the baby. This is your primary concern. You should never let anyone from outside your family unit upset any of you.

Discourage high-maintenance visitors

In the chaos of the first few months, the last thing you need is a high-maintenance visitor like a grandparent who needs special care as well. You can decide to take the bullet for your partner, ask them to visit later, and be branded the bad guy. The important thing is that you keep your flourishing household going smoothly.

Say no to judgment

Some visitors seem to thrive on criticizing everything that you and your partner are doing (or plan to do) in raising your baby. You want to circumcise him? Why, that is barbaric! You want to breastfeed? But the science shows…! Unsolicited advice is a huge no-no for first-time parents. Any visit that leaves you feeling less happy or unsure about your parenting ability is a visit you don't need in the future.

Extended Stays

There is only one way to handle extended stays when you have a baby—you have to approve. Ideally, you actually asked for it because you could really use the help. This is where out-of-work and holidaying siblings come in very handy. Even more importantly, you should only allow long-term visitors who can help out with stuff like laundry, cooking, and other chores. Otherwise, it is just an extra burden that you are putting on your partner and you.

Your Parenting Style

From the onset, you need to determine the kind of parents you will be as a team. Sometimes having a different parenting style from your partner can help your children as they seek guidance in the future, but it also creates room for strife if one parent is permissive and the other is authoritative. At the same time, you do not want to become the father whose style of parenting is "do what your mother says." This all boils down to the kind of adult you want to make of your baby. Attachment styles are formed in infancy. For example, teaching a baby to self-soothe teaches him/her to be independent—a lesson that sticks even later on in life.

As a man, you should avoid becoming too dependent on your mom, sister or other extended family members in determining your parenting style. You can use your own childhood as an inspiration, but the decision you make should be mutually agreeable to both of you.

Ask for guidance

Ultimately, there is someone out there who has a better idea about parenting than you do. Whether it is a member of your family with high-performing children or a parenting expert, there is no problem with asking for help. The important thing is to make sure that you take the decision with your partner as a cohesive unit.

Get help

Help comes in many styles and forms, including books on parenting that are available on the internet. There is absolutely no shame in admitting that you need help. In fact, this admission could be the one thing that saves you from making a huge mistake.

Choose a (authoritative) parenting style and stick to it

There are four parenting styles, namely authoritarian, authoritative, permissive, and uninvolved. Authoritarian parents combine demands for total obedience with low responsiveness to a child's needs while authoritative ones combine high expectations with sufficient support to create a supportive and nurturing environment for the child to grow. On the other hand, permissive parents place very little demands on their children while offering massive support. Finally, uninvolved parents provide neither structure nor support for the child.

Studies indicate that authoritative parenting is the most effective way of raising a child. It facilitates proper growth and maturity in a child academically, socially, emotionally, and personality-wise.

Defend your personality style

Regardless of the studies, there will be people who will question the way you decide to parent your baby. It is important to learn how to defend yourself against these attacks. Or you might decide to disregard the criticism and simply ignore the attacks. Ultimately, it is completely up to you and your partner to decide how you want to raise your child. No one but you has the right to decide (and enforce) your style of parenting.

Chapter 6:

Emotional Bonding and a

Bit of Fun

In all the chapters above, we have looked at the ways through which you can ace being a new daddy by supporting your partner in various activities. Let us now turn our attention to just you and the baby. It is just as important that you create an emotional bond early on. You see, becoming a father isn't just about changing diapers and being the best caregiver, you can be. It also involves fun, precious moments and bonding with your child. In this chapter, we will dive deeper into the topic of paternal bonding. We will look at how the process occurs, what you need to do to hasten it, and ways to make the most of every single experience.

Paternal Detachment

Men and women form parental bonds with their babies in very different ways. For a mom, the relationship has been nine months in the making. The baby has literally been living inside her. The process of birth (labor) further strengthens that relationship. A woman falls in love with her baby from the moment she sets eyes on her. For men, the process takes a little longer. For all intents and purposes, the baby is just another person you have to learn to love. Just because you were so excited about your son's/daughter's birth does not mean that you will fall in love at first sight.

Even if men don't admit to it, not all of them fall in love with the baby from the first instant. Sometimes, you just feel a sense of duty and commitment, but the connection just isn't there. Of course, you would never admit that to a soul because, come on, you are not a monster! But seriously, you are not a bad person just because you don't feel consuming, give-my-life-up-for-you kind of love for your baby initially. As long as you keep working on that emotional bond, everything will be alright. The worst mistake you could ever make is to fail to work on this bond and let your child grow up without that bond. Daddy issues are real and you are now in a position to give your son or daughter his/her future attachment style.

Why Do Dads Have Trouble Connecting

I guess this is the most natural question you would be asking at this point. Why do fathers take so long to bond with their children? Like a lot of issues, this goes back to social norms under which we have developed as humans. In the old days, the role of the father was to protect the bond between the mother and the baby. In that context, fathers were protectors and providers while mothers nurtured the children.

Another explanation is that fathers were the ones who introduced their children to the world when the children were already quite developed. This is why some fathers only start bonding with their children when they start being responsive. While the mother will fall in love with the baby's cute face and tiny fingers, daddies feel a connection when the baby smiles at them or grabs a finger with those tiny hands. I can kind of attest to this theory of interactive bonding. I still remember the emotional shock of feeling my first daughter holding my finger. It was like an emotional jumpstart, reminding me that this little bundle that smelled so new and fresh and felt so precious in my arms was mine... mine!

Obviously, we cannot keep our social interactions as they were hundreds or thousands of years ago when the world was a lot more dangerous and fathers literally had to protect their families from a host of environmental dangers. You have an alarm system now, and the police will be at your home within minutes of any danger. You can stop thinking like a "traditional" man now. If you are feeling somewhat detached, you need to put in the work and foster a strong connection with your baby ASAP.

How to Recognize Your Paternal Detachment

What are some of the things you will be feeling when you are struggling to establish a connection with your baby? Keep in mind that this is not a comprehensive list, and sometimes your detachment will be something that you cannot quite explain.

Reclusiveness

One of the biggest signs of paternal detachment is when you feel like an outsider in your own family. If you feel that you somehow need permission to join your partner when she is bonding with the baby, or you are jealous of her ability to connect so effortlessly, then you are probably dealing with a case of paternal detachment.

You often forget

For the first few days of welcoming the baby into your life, she/he becomes your entire world. Not only will there be friends and family from all over eager for a glimpse and to hold the baby, but the baby supplies will be everywhere. If you have moments when you sort of forget all about the baby, then you are probably not connecting as well as you should.

You are not bothered by the idea of some harm befalling the baby

Does the idea of your baby getting hurt make your blood boil, or does it bring it to a noncommittal simmer? The ugly aspect of paternal detachment is that it nears resentment, especially when the baby causes massive changes and stress in your life.

You miss the good old days of bachelorhood

Would you gladly go back to the time when you were a carefree bachelor? It certainly feels like that carefree time beats the constant crying, the spitting, and the cluelessness of caring for a fussy baby, doesn't it? Sometimes, paternal detachment occurs as a result of stress and sleeplessness in the first frantic days of the baby's birth.

You are not too much bothered by his/her cry

Biologically speaking, women are more attuned to a baby's cry than men. Scientific studies have shown that the male brain remains the same after a baby's cry is heard even when the female brain responds instantly. As I have stated before, this is the main difference in the attachment styles of dads and moms. You have to make a decision to respond (to care) while a mom will respond instinctively. In a way, this makes the bond you form with your baby even more valuable, but it also means that it takes longer to form it.

How to Address Paternal Detachment

There is one very simple strategy to deal with paternal detachment—you have to work to form a bond with your baby. You can start working on the bond even before the baby is born by talking to it in mom's body. If this does not work, then you simply have to work on the relationship after the baby is born.

Strengthening the Paternal Bond

The way to work on fostering a strong bond with your child is by engaging in bonding activities. Instead of moaning that your paternal bond is not as strong as you would like it to be, take a more proactive route and throw yourself at the challenge of falling in love with the baby. In this section, I will highlight eighteen surefire activities to bring you and baby together.

Cuddle Your Baby as Often as Possible

As much as you need to work up your affection towards the baby, you also need to stir that affection in him/her towards you. Babies are usually very attached to their mothers, a result of nine months of close contact followed by breastfeeding and ceaseless doting.

Your opportunity to start establishing a connection starts after birth. Get in as much cradling as you can, including holding the baby in the breastfeeding position as you feed him/her. This gives you ample chances to establish eye contact and a deeper connection. Throw in kisses and smooches as well for full measure. Heavens know that baby's soft skin feels heavenly on your lips.

Get in as Much Skin Contact as Possible

Mothers bond with the baby through skin contact starting from birth and proceeding onwards. You can also nurture your bond with the baby by seeking to establish contact through kisses, bathing, and playtime. Babies enjoy the freedom of being naked, and in a warm enough room, you can play with him/her in a diaper without worrying about giving her a cold. It does help that a baby in diapers looks super cute as well!

Become Baby's Comforter of Second Resort

In the deep of night, when your partner is too tired to wake up to comfort the baby, you will win yourself some important points by becoming the rescuer. You can even have your partner set you up by delaying her response (especially when you are teaching the baby to self-soothe) so that you can come in and save the moment. Your face and your arms should be the next best thing after mommy's face and arms to the baby. Yeah, do not even think about knocking her from the throne. It is impossible.

Make the Baby Laugh

You know that thing about the fun dad—it is well worth a shot. You can take it upon yourself to catalogue all the things that the baby enjoys (those that make her laugh) and those that she doesn't much care for, the ones that elicit nothing above a blank stare. If you are the parent with whom the baby has most fun, you will feel more valuable to the baby and enjoy your time together so much more.

Unlock Your Inner Child With the Baby

You will probably never get a better opportunity to indulge in your most playful tendencies than with your baby. Even though this might not be plausible in the first few months, you can indulge in silly playtime with the baby as much as you like. The better you get at showing your baby a good time, the stronger the bond between you will be even when s/he grows up. Even though your play activities will change over time, the bond will remain just as strong as ever.

Talk to the Baby

You might think that the baby does not understand what you are saying and you are absolutely right, but talking to her goes a long way in nurturing a strong bond between you two. Let your baby become accustomed to your voice. This way, she begins to associate your voice with all the fun activities that you engage in together. Nothing beats receiving an automatic smile from the baby or having him/her extend those tiny hands towards you in eagerness to spend time with you.

Sing

Whether it is jingles or lullabies, songs contain the sounds that elicit the most delightful response to a baby. Singing also makes your voice so much more attractive, making the baby more responsive. Even if she only gives you nothing more than a curious look the first few times, keep on doing it. At some point she will reward you with a smile, then a giggle, and before you know it she will be supporting herself on the bassinet and dancing along to the tune. When the baby goes to sleep to the sound of your voice, it reinforces the bond even further.

Read the Baby a Bedtime Story

The time before sleep is very suitable for strengthening parental bonds with the baby. Read a bedtime story, even if your baby doesn't understand. They'll be soothed by your voice. As your baby develops an attachment to these stories, s/he will also develop an affection for your voice, and in extension, to you.

Watch Your Baby Sleeping

Singing your baby to sleep allows you to establish a stronger bond in him, but watching as he sleeps reinforces the strength of your attachment to the baby. Just imagining how marvelous it is that you formed a full person—mixed in with the cuteness of a sleeping baby—will make you feel more emotional about the baby than you have ever felt before.

Wear the Baby

If you have any negative notions about carrying your baby in a sling, you need to throw them away and get a special sling just for you. More than a stroller, a sling helps you to establish contact with the baby, which is very important in fostering a stronger bond. A sling allows the baby to get used to your smell, your movements, and your touch. It also reinforces the sense of security and safety.

Take Pictures and Family Videos!

Sometimes all you need to do is gaze at the baby through the camera to feel the stirrings of affection. Starting from the hospital bed, you should designate yourself the official cameraman of your small family. Take birth videos, birthday videos, play date videos, record all the firsts, and basically take it upon yourself to document your baby's entire childhood. S/he will be glad to have something with which to relate to those parts of the early life where memories blur as we age. Not to mention the fact that you will have an endless repository of film and pictures to remind yourself of those special moments for you and your partner.

Fill your Role With Grace

When it comes down to it, your baby will probably prefer your partner over you for pretty much all the activities you enjoy doing with him/her. Do not take it personally when the baby cries, fusses, or prefers your partner as a soother. You have a lot of ground to cover to catch up with your partner and you will probably not catch up for years yet. This is not the time for jealousy. The important thing is that your baby is well tended to;

sometimes you just have to accept that you are not the man for the job.

Bath Time Bonding

Babies love playing around with water. As soon as she can, your baby will be splashing and giggling so much during bath time you will probably even forget about the cleaning part. All the fun you have during baths will translate into valuable bonding time for the both of you. As I suggested before, there is great value in carving out bath time as a baby-and-me time.

Dance Together

As soon as the baby can move, you can start dancing together to her favorite music. Even before s/he can move, you can just move around with her/him and trust in the magic of music to do the rest for you.

Try a Baby Massage

There is ample evidence on the benefits of massage in fostering muscle development, soothing tummy aches, and inducing relaxation leading to better sleep in babies. You can take it upon yourself to be your baby's masseuse. A massage provides you with ample opportunities to strengthen the bond with the baby, starting with the skin contact, the simple pleasure of a well-done massage, and the relaxation it gives the baby. Just be careful to apply the lightest touches possible so as not to harm your baby's delicate bone structure. Also use massage oils to reduce the chances of giving the baby friction burns and chafing.

Love on Your Partner in Front of the Baby

Babies can be surprisingly possessive of the people they love. This is why firstborn children have so much trouble accepting the arrival of new siblings. Your baby's first love will be your partner and s/he might be very possessive. In her own little world, mommy's kisses are for her alone. Engaging in some PDA in front of her and then plastering her with smooches is a great way to reinforce the notion of mutual love amongst the three of you.

Take Part in Bedtime Routines

You can decide to partake in any bedtime activities with your partner, but you definitely should never miss out. In fact, bedtime is a great time to reinforce the image of the three of you as a family by loving on each other.

Practice Patience

Patience will become even more of a virtue to you when you are having trouble connecting with your baby. Most of these suggestions take time to bear fruit, and you will probably get a lot of frustrations along the way. However, if you keep at it and never give up, you will one day look and realize that you have long established a deep connection with your baby boy or baby girl. It also helps to think about all these activities in less transactional terms. Sing your baby a lullaby because s/he needs one to soothe them to sleep, not to get a smile or love. Wear the baby because you want to help out, not to get something out of it. Think of it this way—would you be doing any of these things if you had fallen in love with the baby at first sight right from the hospital? You would most probably be doing a lot of these things anyways.

Chapter 7:

Special Circumstances

Of course, fatherhood does not occur uniformly across the board. In an increasingly diverse world, special circumstances abound. It is not strange to find single dads raising babies all on their own, nor do all couples with babies comprise of a man and a woman. In this final chapter, we will examine some circumstances in which a father has to raise a baby alone or deal with challenges that typical couples don't have to worry about.

Dealing With Infertility

The torture of attempting to get a baby but being thwarted by your own body can leave a huge emotional burden in both you and your partner. When the problem is you, it will be even harder to deal with the fact that you cannot father your own child and will have to opt for alternative methods. If you do not find a healthy way of dealing with the whole situation, it might have a really negative impact on not just your relationship, but your own mental well-being as well. In this section, we will look at some of the most effective strategies for dealing with infertility.

Process Your Emotions

I get that infertility makes you feel vulnerable and you don't like it (who does?) but you really need to deal with it. You are probably very sad about not being able to conceive your own son/daughter or stressed about alternative methods of conception that you have to use. Regardless of how bleak the situation seems from your point of view, there will always be a way out. However, if you let your emotions get in the way of your logical thinking, you will not be able to see it.

You need to have an honest talk with someone, anyone, about how you are feeling. Prominent among your emotions right now will be emasculation, and you might be overcompensating by acting all macho and invulnerable so you might respond with hostility to suggestions for help. Studies indicate that men who have been struggling to impregnate their partner and those who have to resort to alternative means are more likely to exhibit classical "manly" personality traits like invincibility. In most cases, men do this because society has this idea that a man is supposed to hold his emotions back and take control. So, when your partner is expressing her frustration (and thus getting a chance to deal with her feelings), you continue ignoring your own because you feel that you have got to hold yourself together.

Deal With It as a Couple

If you have been trying to get pregnant with your partner for a while, then you should have realized by now that you are in it together. Your partner is probably going through the same emotional rollercoaster that you are going through, so she understands perfectly. Understand that it is a couple's problem requiring a united front. Even as you deal with your hurt male pride, keep in mind that your partner also has emotions to deal with. Be as considerate to her feelings as you can without ignoring your own emotions.

Whatever happens, two people will be affected. If you have to find an alternative method to get her pregnant, if you have to find a surrogate mother, or if you will resort to adopting a baby, it is all happening to you. You must both understand what any necessary changes mean to your relationship.

Do Not Fixate

Whatever you do about your fertility problem, you had better do it sooner rather than later. The more you dwell on the problem and the more you consider the repercussions of infertility, the more stressed out you will become and the more your emotional well-being is likely to take a dip. Asking yourself why over and over again will only make you frozen with inaction and helplessness. If you are not careful, it might even descend into depression and take a serious toll on your relationship.

Instead, ask yourself what you can do. The important thing when you are seeking to become a father is raising a child and watching her/him grow up to become a self-sufficient adult. Even if you miss out on the opportunity to pass on your DNA to the next generation, you can still father a child. Just because the child you raise does not carry your DNA will not make you any less of a father. In fact, it might be just what you need to appreciate the really important aspects of parenting.

Come up With an Action Plan

As you turn your mind away from the tragic situation of your infertility, you should start coming up with concrete ideas. If you are the one with infertility issues, you need to find out if your problem is conceiving through natural sex or it is your virility that is too low. If you can use natural insemination, then go with that. If not, consider what your partner needs. If she cares about pregnancy, you can get a sperm donor to help out. If not, you can get a surrogate mother or just adopt. With the former, you will both be participating in the pregnancy as outsiders with a vested interest.

On the other hand, if your partner is the one with fertility issues, again it depends on whether artificial methods of conception can help. You should try as much as possible to use solutions that give you and your partner a greater role in the conception and the in-utero growth of the baby. It is not a qualifying factor, but having a child that shares your DNA does have a certain biological edge to just adopting. It gives you greater investment in the baby. At the same time, adoption allows you to play a part in providing a home for an unfortunate child, which can be pretty fulfilling as well. Mull over your possibilities and choose the most practical solution to your problem.

Try Natural Solutions

Sometimes the cause of infertility is the wrong kind of lifestyle messing up with the body's ability to produce healthy sperm. By working on your body, you will also be improving your physical ability to procreate, not to mention the positive impact of the following recommended actions on the mind.

Eat right

One of the most effective ways of dealing with common male fertility issues like sperm motility is surprisingly simple—follow a diet consisting of only lean meat, whole grains, and veggies. Diet changes are quite effective even though they only require very slight shifts in your general lifestyle.

Lose weight

In recent studies, nutritionists have discovered strong links between obesity and reduced levels of fertility in men. If you are overweight, working on bringing your weight down might be just the thing you need to turn things around.

Avoid stress

Recent evidence points to a huge correlation between stress and fertility. Stressing over your infertility might indeed be making your inability to reproduce worse. If you are dealing with this problem, you should consider using the physical activity and other healthy habits described above. The more you are doing to take charge and turn the situation around, the better you will feel about the whole situation, and thus the greater your ability to turn it all around.

Single Parenthood

A single mother will have difficulties coping with some of the aspects of raising a child, but a single father will struggle with pretty much ALL of them. Depending on the stage of the baby's development at which you start your single parenthood, you will face a range of challenges that might make your life very complicated. In this section, we will look at some of the things that you can do to cope with the burden of raising a child when the mother is not around.

At any stage of the baby's development, being a single dad has different challenges depending on the way that your single parenthood came about. Maybe you won custody from your partner in a divorce settlement, or your girlfriend decided to leave the baby with you after a breakup. In the worst-case scenario, you become a single father after the death of your partner. The situation in which you became a single father will determine the level of emotional upheaval that you go through. The more tragic the situation, the worse off you will be. In the event of death of the partner, the emotional toll of taking care of the baby—seeing your partner in him/her at every moment—can get really disturbing.

Another factor is the stage at which you get the baby. Lacking the nurturing instinct that mothers use to get babies to breastfeed early in life, men struggle with basic baby care chores like feeding and soothing. If the baby is still young enough to require that you do everything for him/her, you will also be quite physically exhausted if you have to do everything alone. Your finances will also take a bigger dip because you cannot count on your partner's contribution to the baby care expenses.

Find Effective Ways to Deal With the Stress

Whether you have become a single father through divorce, death of a partner, or other circumstances, chances are that your first few experiences of dealing with the baby alone are going to be very stressful. Compounded with the stress of losing your partner, you might find that you have a tough time just functioning, let alone caring for the baby. Yet it is very important that you pull yourself together because the only worse thing for the baby would be to lose both parents. Do not get lost in your remorse. Instead, find a proper outlet for it—sporting activities, hobbies, therapy, etc.—and keep on caring for your baby. It is very important that you recognize those feelings of loss and hurt. There are no widely accepted social norms for guys raising kids alone, so you will not have a lot of know-how to work with. So, here is an important piece of advice: take care of yourself first and foremost.

Get Support

There is a huge difference between help and support. With the former, you will have someone who helps you to perform tasks but little emotional care. With support, you have people willing to offer their help who also understand your situation and empathize. It is this second kind of help that will be most useful in single parenthood. So try not to withdraw from your friends and family, however much you feel like retreating into your shell and hiding from the world. Your responsibility to the child trumps any personal pride that you might have. Family support allows you to deal with the issue at hand as well as working out your emotions, which will most probably be all over the place when you are a single dad trying to raise a son/daughter alone.

Another important kind of support you will need is emotional support for dealing with the special challenges that single fatherhood brings. You can find a support group (even if it's just an online community) where you can share your frustrations and ask for assistance. Like I mentioned above, there isn't much precedent for raising a child as a single father, especially from a young age. The people in your support group will, at the very least, relate with your special brand of life challenges.

Create a Routine

The biggest problem with single parenthood is usually the breakdown of the family structure. The least you can do is create an environment that reinforces stability and permanence through things like a routine and structured home life. You will have to work extra hard to meet your baby's social, physical, and emotional needs. You have to find the perfect balance between the father's role or protection and guidance and the mother's role as the compassionate and nurturing parent. It is no doubt going to be a lot of work, but it will be fulfilling and satisfactory work. Your reward will be the joy of watching your child grow and mature under your sole care. And even though this satisfaction will only come after years and years of hard work, it will be well worth the effort.

One Baby, Two Dads

There are a few options available for gay couples looking to have a baby. You can choose to get a surrogate mother, adopt a baby, foster one, or find someone with whom you can become co-parents. On the whole, the process of fatherhood will probably be very challenging for you. For one thing, following the surrogacy process to have someone have the baby for you will be very expensive. Another challenge you might face is the legal hurdles along the process. In this section, we will look at some of the common problems you can expect to deal with when you are in a gay relationship and you are trying to father a baby.

Prepare Emotionally

The fact that you are in a monogamous relationship and can only have a baby through someone else makes the moment when you welcome your baby into your lives even more special. Another area where you will need to prepare—by fortifying yourself emotionally—will be in dealing with societal persecution. As much as gay marriage has gained support in most countries in the world, there is still a lot of disapproval. Your child will be different from all his/her friends and you must make sure that you prepare them for being ostracized.

One of the most effective ways of ensuring that your son/daughter feels like they belong, even when they are being bullied, is to have a circle of friends and family supporting their growth and development. The more diverse the support they get early on, the bigger their sense of belonging will be.

Assign Roles

Same-sex couples do not have the same kind of clearly demarcated roles that heterogeneous couples have. You will have to share the parenting roles that lie ahead a lot more equally because no one can claim to have a biological advantage in any area. As such, you will have to assign roles based on how good you are at different areas of the baby's care.

However, you will also have to assign supporting feminine roles like godmothers and role models a lot more carefully. You should opt for lifelong friends and/or family members—relationships with a higher probability of lasting for life. This helps to avoid any future possibility of soured relations leading to upheaval for your child.

Work out the Legal Issues

Different countries have different laws regarding parenting for gay couples. For example, Australian surrogacy laws do not compel a mother to give up their child unless you had entered into a paid agreement. Different states in the United States have different adoption laws regarding same-sex couples. Make sure that you familiarize yourself with your region's bylaws regarding gay parenting before starting the process of fatherhood. A trustworthy adoption lawyer is one of the most stress-free means of ensuring that you get all your issues well addressed ahead of time.

Enjoy Your Fatherhood

Other than the issues discussed in this section, there is no distinction between gay parenthood and the traditional kind of raising a family. All the rules and tips discussed in the entirety of this book apply to you just as much as they apply to a man in a heterosexual relationship. Do not let anything or anyone come in the way of you becoming the best dad in the world.

Conclusion

Regardless of the kind of situation through which you are becoming a father, you should start preparing for this eventuality long before conception. To strengthen the bond between you and the baby, become as involved as you possibly can in the growth and development process of the baby during pregnancy. This means attending doctor's appointments, going with your partner to birthing classes, and working on the more physically demanding preparations like baby-proofing the house and working on the nursery.

Through the course of the pregnancy, your partner will go through different phases of physical and emotional changes. You can expect to go through massive changes to the relationship, including how you engage in sexual activity. You will either have a partner with a stronger sex drive throughout the pregnancy, one whose sexual drive decreases as the pregnancy advances, one with a reduced one throughout, or one that fluctuates as the months go by. You should make sure that you flow with the tide and avoid making your partner feel pressured either way.

However much you try, you will never understand how it feels to have a baby growing inside you. That is why the man's job during pregnancy is always to support his partner in whatever she is going through. Worry about things like the nursery and baby-proofing the house so that she does not have to do it.

In preparation for the baby's birth, it is important that you have a serious discussion with your partner as to the kind of birth you are going to have. Natural birth is recommended for any woman who can pull it off because it gives the best recovery time for the woman and has some very useful benefits for the child. To settle on the best one, sit down for an honest, professionally guided talk with your doctor well in advance of the birth. You should also talk with your partner about your role in the birth. There are great benefits to participating in the birth of your baby, prominent among which is an improved ability to bond with your baby early on and lending much-needed support to your partner through this stressful time.

But whether you participate in the delivery directly or not, your role will be that of a committed assistant from the onset of labor to the arrival of your baby into the universe. Worry about things like the hospital bag so that she does not have to do it. You should also be the buffer between your partner and friends and family who come to lend their support during and after labor. You should also be your partner's advocate among the delivery staff. Ensure that the delivery goes how you and your partner envisioned it, even if others oppose.

In the early days of your baby's arrival at home, you will find yourself getting overwhelmed with chores and endless tasks. However, the most important moments will be those entailing direct care for the baby. Even though you will struggle to do it right in the first few weeks or so, you will find a lot of joy in activities like bathing, feeding, and dressing up the baby. You will probably find some of the other activities like changing the diaper and burping the baby hard to master and rather disgusting (ew, poop!), but they are just as important for establishing a connection with your baby.

Speaking of which, some fathers struggle to connect with their babies in the first few days. This is quite normal, but it does not mean that you have to accept it. You might find yourself dealing with paternal detachment, a condition that affects quite a large number of men and affects the amount of affection between daddy and baby. If you find any excuse to avoid spending time with the baby, you wish for the old stress-free days, or you envy the relationship between your partner and the baby, then chances are that you haven't formed a very strong bond with the baby yet.

You should engage in nurturing and play activities with the baby as much as possible to make sure that you build your relationship and that you fall in love with the baby. The only thing a father is supposed to feel about his daughter/son is overpowering love and protectiveness. Resentment and indifference have no place in this very special bond.

Sometimes the reason why you are not having any success bonding with your baby is because you have not dealt with the emotions their birth evokes in you. Dealing with excitement, helplessness, joy, spousal emotional distance, and an outpouring of issues from your own childhood can be rather taxing emotionally. Especially if you do not deal with your childhood emotional baggage, you will find it very difficult to bond. In these times, you will be more like a child and less like the father, which will further complicate the relationship. You have to deal with these emotions so that you can deal with any red flags holding you back from being a great parent.

Another mistake a lot of fathers make is ignoring their postpartum depression even when it continues to wreak havoc on their emotional and mental well-being. If the birth of your baby did not give you joy, or if you are feeling frustrated and exhibiting the signs of violence, you should seek help as soon as possible. However, to do this, you must first overcome the stigma. As much as you are expected to be a "man" you must now keep in mind that you are someone's father. You have to take care of your emotional well-being and throw off some of those stereotypes about manhood that you have been holding on to.

Do not be surprised if your relationship with your mate takes the backseat in the weeks and months following the baby's birth. However, do not accept this as the new normal. You must keep working on the older relationship because it directly impacts the emotional well-being of the baby.

It is inevitable that family and friends will be very interested in the birth of your child. And as your wife puts in much of the work, you will have to learn how to deal with all the family members and friends who will visit your home to wish you well. Most importantly, you will have to strike the perfect balance between letting them in and preserving the familial bonds you have established with your partner and your child. You will also have to learn how to defend your parenting style against people who disagree and those who will criticize you.

The final piece of advice I have for you is how to deal with special circumstances. The most common include dealing with infertility, single fatherhood, and gay parenting. In the first scenario, the most important thing is to find a way forward and follow through on it as a couple. Avoid blaming each other and go into whatever solution you decide to use as a couple with as much excitement as you would embrace a traditional childbearing situation. With single parenthood, the two most important things that you must do is deal with your emotions regarding the absence of the mother as well as how to utilize the help of friends and family. With gay fatherhood, make sure that you assign roles in advance and create a strong support system around your baby.

So, there you have it—the most comprehensive guide on fatherhood that you will find anywhere on the internet. As promised, I have tackled those uniquely male issues that fathers encounter in the process of procreating. There is nothing difficult about it. In fact, it can be a pretty exciting time for you, your partner, and your baby. As long as you are willing to put in the time and effort, you will easily become the perfect example of fatherhood for everyone around you. And most importantly, you will be literally the best daddy in the world for your son/daughter right at his/her birth.

Thank you for walking with me through this journey. It gives me enormous pleasure to have the opportunity to pass on all the knowledge I have accumulated over the years pertaining to baby care for daddies. I also hope that you find this book enlightening enough to warrant a favorable review. Help me get this information to first time daddies everywhere!

References

Dads: 10 ways to be the perfect birth partner. (n.d.). Retrieved from https://www.babycentre.co.uk/a1072/dads-10-ways-to-be-the-perfect-birth-partner

For Expecting Dads and Partners. (2020, March 13). Retrieved from https://www.whattoexpect.com/pregnancy/expecting-father/

Labor & Delivery Support Tips Just For Dads. (n.d.). Retrieved from https://www.parents.com/pregnancy/giving-birth/labor-support/labor-delivery-advice-dads/

New dad: Tips to help manage stress. (2020, March 11). Retrieved from https://www.mayoclinic.org/healthy-lifestyle/infant-and-toddler-health/in-depth/new-dad/art-20045880

Made in the USA
San Bernardino, CA
10 June 2020